Samson Agonistes
and
Shorter Poems

Crofts Classics

GENERAL EDITOR

Samuel H. Beer, *Harvard University*

JOHN MILTON

Samson Agonistes
and
Shorter Poems

EDITED BY

A. E. Barker

UNIVERSITY OF WESTERN ONTARIO

Harlan Davidson, Inc.
Arlington Heights, Illinois 60004

Library of Congress Cataloging-in-Publication Data

Milton, John, 1608–1674.
　　Samson Agonistes, and other shorter poems.

　　(Crofts classics)
　　Bibliography: p.
　　1. Samson (Biblical judge)—Poetry.　I. Barker,
Arthur Edward, 1911–　　.　II. Title.
PR3552.B25　1987　　　822′.4　　　　87-7417
ISBN 0-88295-058-4 (pbk.)

Manufactured in the United States of America
95　94　93　　　　　　　　34 CM

CONTENTS

INTRODUCTION

THIS volume contains the principal English poems of Milton's youth and early manhood, most of the sonnets written during the Puritan Revolution when he was chiefly engaged in arguing public questions in prose, and *Samson Agonistes*, published three years before his death. The early poems are often studied for their handling of themes treated in epic proportions in *Paradise Lost* or as records of Milton's development and the progressive formulation of his conception of his function as a Christian poet. They deserve to be read simply for themselves, as among the final productions of the English Renaissance with its poetically powerful combination of faith, high idealism, heroic morality, urbanity, expansive imagination, and pagan sensuousness, expressed in a language still flexible in its youth but firm in its new maturity. In some of Milton's earlier and slighter poems characteristic Renaissance qualities appear separately. In "L'Allegro" and "Il Penseroso" the meditative mind in its cheerful and pensive moods ranges, with an urbanity rare in Milton, over many of the subjects attractive to the Renaissance imagination. "At a Solemn Music" and the sonnet "How soon hath Time" mark out the path of self-dedicated religious and moral discipline which led through the prose to the great poems. Yet, like those later works, the most impressive of the early pieces fuse many Renaissance qualities. "Christs Nativity" combines traditionally Christian with pagan conceptions and symbols to express the significance of the Incarnation through an art both charmingly youthful and highly organized. "Comus," the most ambitious of these pieces, develops a high-souled ethical theme in opposition to "carnal sensualty," but remains a delightful masque, urbanely and gracefully complimentary in the conventional manner of courtly entertainment and as varied in its beauty as the virtue it attempts to characterize. "Lycidas," in structural precision and variety of detail and music the consummate achievement of the early period, employs the delicately artificial conventions of classical pastoral elegy as a framework for the expression of Milton's deepest moral and religious convictions. The early poems everywhere illustrate the conjunction of the sensuous and other-worldly, the pagan and religious, the natural and spiritual, which is the special mark of Milton's genius and of the Renaissance tradition of classical and Christian humanism.

In a chastened form, this tradition provides *Samson Agonistes* with its concentrated power. Between the early poems and that drama lay Milton's experience of a revolution animated by moral idealism and ending in shameful anarchy and defeat. The quality of this experience—of public infamy and anger, of thwarted political and religious hopes, of personal suffering in blindness and loneliness sustained with fortitude and some measure of urbanity—is indicated by the sonnets, each tensely-wrought unit expressing a facet of Milton's personality. *Samson Agonistes* is sometimes read as an account of this experience, for the blind and aging Samson, isolated in misery, sensible at once of weakness and failure and of the divine sanction of his apparently defeated cause, strikingly resembles Milton after the Restoration. But the drama is far more than autobiographical. In Milton intense personal emotion revitalizes and reshapes traditional symbols, poetic forms, and readings of experience, to issue in universally significant works of coherent art. Whatever is personal to him in the drama is merged into its presentation of the agony or struggle through which Samson, already in Christian tradition a type of Christ and so of every Christian in a hostile world, achieves self-mastery in temptation and triumph in defeat. To concentrate attention on Samson's struggle and to develop its complex meaning Milton uses the impersonal and simple conventions of Greek tragedy (described in his preface and very different from the conventions of Shakespearean tragedy), and in particular its convention of choral comment, questioning, and enlightenment. *Samson Agonistes* is without the rich variety of the early poems; but it is profoundly impressive in the severe beauty of its art, the intensity of its spiritual conflict, the fusion of the biblical and classical through which its central figure emerges as both suffering servant and suffering hero, and the hard-won confidence of its commentary on man's ways and God's.

Revisionary expansion of this volume's selected bibliography (by over a third) prompts the additional comment that criticism of Milton has been much concerned in the past fifteen years with the interrelation of classical and Christian in his art and reading of experience. Critics have clarified his manipulation, in early and later poems and not least in *Samson*, of typological and figural modes drawn from Scripture. This has made more intelligible his sympathetic or ironic response to such traditional patterns and their implications for experience. Some critics have attempted to express our increased sense of his subtlety of art and meaning in terms of the renewed tradition of devotional meditation in his time. Others find a significant relation, not least as to music, with the spiritualized classicism of the baroque and even mannerist art of the period. While some think this newly recognized complexity symptomatic of conflict, others see in it the representation of a unified reading of the pattern of a vitally human and spiritual experience. Differences of opinion about the essentials of this, and about the relation of the natural and spiritual in it, are illustrated by sharp differences of emphasis—on the mystical, rational, sensuous, experiential, existential—in the early poems and in *Samson*, with the New-Testament implications of its representation of an Old-Testament story, through the adaptation of classical effects and complex echoes of Biblical patterns of imagery, phrasing, thought, belief. But the critical development suggested by the enlargement of the bibliography has deepened our sense of the continued relevance of Milton's response to the crucial vitality of human experience, as he saw this in the response to God's ways he thought open to men in theirs, and as he poetically represented it.

PRINCIPAL DATES IN THE LIFE
OF JOHN MILTON

❧

1608 Born in Bread Street, London, December 9.

1616 *Death of William Shakespeare.*

1625 Entered Christ's College Cambridge. *Accession of Charles I.*

1629 Bachelor of Arts.

1632 Master of Arts. Studying at his father's house at Horton, Buckinghamshire, until April, 1638.

1638-39 Travelled in Italy, returning to settle in London and teach private pupils.

1639 *First Bishops' War against the Scots over church discipline.*

1640 *Second Bishops' War. Opening of the Long Parliament. Root and Branch Petition for the abolition of episcopacy in England.*

1641-42 Five pamphlets by Milton in favor of church reform.

1642 Married Mary Powell. *Beginning of the Civil War.*

1643 *Parliament appointed the Westminster Assembly of Divines to settle the reformed government of the church.*

1644-45 Four pamphlets by Milton urging reform of divorce laws.

1644 *Of Education. Areopagitica.*

1645 *Royalists defeated at Naseby.*

1645-46   *Poems . . . , Both English and Latin.*

1648-51   *War between Parliament and the Scots.*

1649   *Execution of Charles I.* Political writings by Milton. Appointed Secretary for Foreign Tongues to the Council of State.

1651   *Pro Populo Anglicano Defensio.*

1652   Total blindness, followed by progressive retirement from official duties. Death of Mary Milton.

1653   *Oliver Cromwell became Lord Protector.*

1654   *Pro Populo Anglicano Defensio Secunda.*

1656   Married Katherine Woodcock.

1658   Death of Katherine Milton. *Death of Oliver. Succession of Richard Cromwell as Protector.*

1659   *Abdication of Richard Cromwell, followed by political anarchy.* Two pamphlets by Milton on religious liberty.

1660   *The Readie and Easie Way to Establish a Free Commonwealth* and other political writings by Milton. *Restoration of the monarchy and return of Charles II.* Milton briefly imprisoned.

1661-62   *The regicide judges and Sir Henry Vane executed.*

1663   Married Elizabeth Minshull.

1667   *Paradise Lost.*

1671   *Paradise Regained, Samson Agonistes.*

1673   New and enlarged edition of *Poems* (of 1645).

1674   Second edition of *Paradise Lost.* Died, November 8.

SHORTER POEMS OF JOHN MILTON

On the Morning of Christs Nativity

I

THIS is the Month, and this the happy morn
Wherin the Son of Heav'ns eternal King,
Of wedded Maid, and Virgin Mother born,
Our great redemption from above did bring;
For so the holy sages once did sing,
    That he our deadly forfeit should release,
And with his Father work us a perpetual peace.

II

That glorious Form, that Light unsufferable,
And that far-beaming blaze of Majesty,
Wherwith he wont at Heav'ns high Councel-Table,   10
To sit the midst of Trinal Unity,
He laid aside; and here with us to be,
    Forsook the Courts of everlasting Day,
And chose with us a darksom House of mortal Clay.

III

Say Heav'nly Muse, shall not thy sacred vein
Afford a present to the Infant God?
Hast thou no vers, no hymn, or solemn strein,
To welcom him to this his new abode,
Now while the Heav'n by the Suns team untrod,
    Hath took no print of the approching light,   20
And all the spangled host keep watch in squadrons bright?

IV

See how from far upon the Eastern rode
The Star-led Wisards haste with odours sweet:

Where no other indication is given in the notes, the text through-
out is from *Poems,* 1645.

5 **sages** prophets 6 **deadly forfeit** penalty of death for sin
10 **wont** used

1

O run, prevent them with thy humble ode,
And lay it lowly at his blessed feet;
Have thou the honour first, thy Lord to greet,
    And joyn thy voice unto the Angel Quire,
From out his secret Altar toucht with hallow'd fire.

Sun, dawn

THE HYMN

I

It was the Winter wilde,
30 While the Heav'n-born-childe,
    All meanly wrapt in the rude manger lies;
Nature in aw to him
Had doff't her gawdy trim,
    With her great Master so to sympathize:
It was no season then for her
To wanton with the Sun her lusty Paramour.

II

Onely with speeches fair
She woo's the gentle Air
    To hide her guilty front with innocent Snow,
40 And on her naked shame,
Pollute with sinfull blame,
    The Saintly Vail of Maiden white to throw,
Confounded, that her Makers eyes
Should look so neer upon her foul deformities.

III

But he her fears to cease,
Sent down the meek-eyd Peace,
    She crown'd with Olive green, came softly sliding
Down through the turning sphear
His ready Harbinger,
50   With Turtle wing the amorous clouds dividing,
And waving wide her mirtle wand,
She strikes a universall Peace through Sea and Land.

24 **prevent** arrive before 28 Isaiah vi: 6, 7. 36 **wanton** gambol
Paramour lover 39 **front** forehead, face 48 **sphear** globe of uni-
verse 49 **Harbinger** forerunner 50 **Turtle** turtle-dove

IV

No War, or Battails sound
Was heard the World around:
 The idle spear and shield were high up hung;
The hooked Chariot stood
Unstain'd with hostile blood,
 The Trumpet spake not to the armed throng,
And Kings sate still with awfull eye,
As if they surely knew their sovran Lord was by. 60

V

But peacefull was the night
Wherin the Prince of light
 His raign of peace upon the earth began:
The Windes with wonder whist,
Smoothly the waters kist,
 Whispering new joyes to the milde Ocean,
Who now hath quite forgot to rave,
While Birds of Calm sit brooding on the charmed wave.

VI

The Stars with deep amaze
Stand fixt in stedfast gaze, 70
 Bending one way their pretious influence,
And will not take their flight,
For all the morning light,
 Or *Lucifer* that often warn'd them thence;
But in their glimmering Orbs did glow,
Untill their Lord himself bespake, and bid them go.

VII

And though the shady gloom
Had given day her room,
 The Sun himself with-held his wonted speed,
And hid his head for shame, 80
As his inferiour flame,
 The new-enlightn'd world no more should need;

56 **hooked** with scythe-like hooks on the hubs 59 **awful** rever-
ent 64 **whist** hushed 68 **Birds of Calm** halcyons, thought by the
Greeks to breed on the calm sea in December during the year's
longest nights and shortest days 71 **influence** power to affect hu-
man affairs 74 **Lucifer** morning star

He saw a greater Sun appear
Then his bright Throne, or burning Axletree could bear.

VIII

The Shepherds on the Lawn,
Or ere the point of dawn,
   Sate simply chatting in a rustick row;
Full little thought they than,
That the mighty *Pan*
90   Was kindly com to live with them below;
Perhaps their loves, or els their sheep,
Was all that did their silly thoughts so busie keep.

IX

When such musick sweet
Their hearts and ears did greet,
   As never was by mortall finger strook,
Divinely-warbled voice
Answering the stringed noise,
   As all their souls in blisfull rapture took:
The Air such pleasure loth to lose,
100 With thousand echo's still prolongs each heav'nly close.

X

Nature that heard such sound
Beneath the hollow round
   Of *Cynthia's* seat, the Airy region thrilling,
Now was almost won
To think her part was don,
   And that her raign had here its last fulfilling;
She knew such harmony alone
Could hold all Heav'n and Earth in happier union.

XI

At last surrounds their sight
110 A Globe of circular light,
   That with long beams the shame-fac't night array'd,
The helmed Cherubim

85 **Lawn** meadow 86 **Or ere** before 88 **than** then 89 **Pan** Greek
nature god and shepherd of stars, associated from early Chris-
tian times with the Good Shepherd 92 **silly** innocent 100 **close**
cadence 102 **round** sphere 103 **Cynthia** moon goddess

And sworded Seraphim,
  Are seen in glittering ranks with wings displaid,
Harping in loud and solemn quire,
With unexpressive notes to Heav'ns new-born Heir.

XII

Such Musick (as 'tis said)
Before was never made,
  But when of old the sons of morning sung,
While the Creator Great   120
His constellations set,
  And the well-ballanc't world on hinges hung,
And cast the dark foundations deep,
And bid the weltring waves their oozy channel keep.

XIII

Ring out ye Crystall sphears,
Once bless our human ears,
  (If ye have power to touch our senses so)
And let your silver chime
Move in melodious time;
  And let the Base of Heav'ns deep Organ blow,   130
And with your ninefold harmony
Make up full consort to th'Angelike symphony.

XIV

For if such holy Song
Enwrap our fancy long,
  Time will run back, and fetch the age of gold,
And speckl'd vanity

116 **unexpressive** inexpressible 117-24 Job xxvi: 7, xxxvii: 6-ठ
122 **hinges** supports 125-32 The moon, planets (including the
sun), and stars seemed to the ancients to move upon nine sep-
arate spheres with earth as their fixed centre, according to the
Ptolemaic astronomy accepted in modified forms until displaced
by the sun-centred Copernican system in the sixteenth and sev-
enteenth centuries. As it moved each sphere was thought to pro-
duce a musical note, the notes making up a perfect harmony
which, according to the Greek philosopher, Pythagoras, men
might have heard had they been wholly virtuous, a notion devel-
oped by Plato in his *Republic*, X, 616-17. See Milton's "Second
Academic Exercise" and "Paradise Lost," VIII, 1-178. 135 **age
of gold** in Greek legend remote age of perfect men when the
gods dwelt upon the earth

Will sicken soon and die,
    And leprous sin will melt from earthly mould,
And Hell it self will pass away,
140 And leave her dolorous mansions to the peering day.

XV

Yea Truth, and Justice then
Will down return to men,
    Orb'd in a Rain-bow; and like glories wearing
Mercy will sit between,
Thron'd in Celestiall sheen,
    With radiant feet the tissued clouds down stearing,
And Heav'n as at som festivall,
Will open wide the Gates of her high Palace Hall.

XVI

But wisest Fate sayes no,
150 This must not yet be so,
    The Babe lies yet in smiling Infancy,
That on the bitter cross
Must redeem our loss;
    So both himself and us to glorifie:
Yet first to those ychain'd in sleep,
The wakefull trump of doom must thunder through the
    deep,

XVII

With such a horrid clang
As on mount *Sinai* rang
    While the red fire, and smouldring clouds out brake:
160 The aged Earth agast
With terrour of that blast,
    Shall from the surface to the center shake;
When at the worlds last session,
The dreadfull Judge in middle Air shall spread his throne.

XVIII

And then at last our bliss
Full and perfect is,
    But now begins; for from this happy day

141-44 Psalms LXXXV: 10-11 143-44 **Orb'd . . . between** *1673;
1645 reads*: "Th' enameld *Arras* of the Rainbow wearing, /And
Mercy set between,/" 157-59 Exodus XIX: 16-20

Th'old Dragon under ground
In straiter limits bound,
   Not half so far casts his usurped sway,   170
And wrath to see his Kingdom fail,
Swindges the scaly Horrour of his foulded tail.

XIX

The Oracles are dumm,
No voice or hideous humm
   Runs through the arched roof in words deceiving.
Apollo from his shrine
Can no more divine,
   With hollow shreik the steep of *Delphos* leaving.
No nightly trance, or breathed spell,
Inspire's the pale-ey'd Priest from the prophetic cell.   180

XX

The lonely mountains o're,
And the resounding shore,
   A voice of weeping heard, and loud lament;
From haunted spring, and dale
Edg'd with poplar pale.
   The parting Genius is with sighing sent,
With flowre-inwov'n tresses torn
The Nimphs in twilight shade of tangled thickets mourn.

XXI

In consecrated Earth,
And on the holy Hearth,   190
   The *Lars*, and *Lemures* moan with midnight plaint,
In Urns, and Altars round,
A drear, and dying sound
   Affrights the *Flamins* at their service quaint;
And the chill Marble seems to sweat,
While each peculiar power forgoes his wonted seat.

168 **Dragon** Satan, Revelation xii: 172 **Swindges** swings violently 173 **Oracles** ambiguous prophecies obtained at the shrines of pagan gods, whose power to prophesy ended according to Christian tradition at the time of Christ's birth 176 **Apollo** Greek god of sun, poetry, music 177 **divine** predict 186 **Genius** god of a locality 191 **Lars** household gods **Lemures** ancestral spirits 194 **Flamins** pagan priests **quaint** elaborate

XXII

Peor, and *Baalim,*
Forsake their Temples dim,
   With that twise batter'd god of *Palestine,*
200 And mooned *Ashtaroth,*
Heav'ns Queen and Mother both,
   Now sits not girt with Tapers holy shine,
The Libyc *Hammon* shrinks his horn,
In vain the *Tyrian* Maids their wounded *Thamuz* mourn.

XXIII

And sullen *Moloch* fled,
Hath left in shadows dred,
   His burning Idol all of blackest hue,
In vain with Cymbals ring,
They call the grisly king,
210   In dismall dance about the furnace blue,
The brutish gods of *Nile* as fast,
Isis and *Orus,* and the Dog *Anubis* hast.

XXIV

Nor is *Osiris* seen
In *Memphian* Grove, or Green,
   Trampling the unshowr'd Grasse with lowings loud:
Nor can he be at rest
Within his sacred chest,
   Naught but profoundest Hell can be his shroud,
In vain with Timbrel'd Anthems dark
220 The sable-stoled Sorcerers bear his worship Ark.

XXV

He feels from *Juda*'s Land
The dredded Infants hand,
   The rayes of *Bethlehem* blind his dusky eyn;

197 **Peor, Baalim** Canaanite gods 199 **twise batter'd god** Dagon,
Philistine god; *I* Samuel v: 4 200 **Ashtaroth** moon goddess of
Phoenicians 203 **Libyc Hammon** Egyptian god, a horned ram
204 **Thamuz** Phoenician (Tyrian) god of summer, slain by a boar
representing winter 205 **Moloch** Semitic deity worshipped with
human sacrifices by fire 212 **Isis, Orus, Anubis** Egyptian deities,
partly animal 213 **Osiris** god of the Nile, supposed incarnate as
the sacred bull of Memphis and sometimes represented as a
mummy 218 **shroud** shelter 220 **sable-stoled** black-robed

Nor all the gods beside,
Longer dare abide,
    Not *Typhon* huge ending in snaky twine:
Our Babe to shew his Godhead true,
Can in his swadling bands controul the damned crew.

XXVI

So when the Sun in bed,
Curtain'd with cloudy red,   230
    Pillows his chin upon an Orient wave,
The flocking shadows pale,
Troop to th'infernall jail,
    Each fetter'd Ghost slips to his severall grave,
And the yellow-skirted *Fayes,*
Fly after the Night-steeds, leaving the Moon-lov'd maze.

XXVII

But see the Virgin blest,   } *Virgin's part is over*
Hath laid her Babe to rest.
    Time is our tedious Song should here have ending:
Heav'ns youngest teemed Star,   240
Hath fixt her polisht Car,
    Her sleeping Lord with Handmaid Lamp attending.
And all about the Courtly Stable,
Bright-harnest Angels sit in order serviceable.

                                                    1629

On Shakespear

WHAT needs my *Shakespear* for his honour'd Bones,
The labour of an age in piled Stones,
Or that his hallow'd reliques should be hid
Under a Star-ypointing *Pyramid?*
Dear son of memory, great heir of Fame,
What need'st thou such weak witnes of thy name?
Thou in our wonder and astonishment

226 **Typhon** Greek earth-monster, serpent below the waist, man above, slain by Hercules 232 **shadows** spirits 235 **severall** separate 237 **Night-steeds** horses drawing the chariot of night 240 **youngest teemed** latest born 244 **harnest** armored 5 **son of memory** because remembered and because the Greeks represented the Muses of the various arts as daughters of Memory

Hast built thy self a live-long Monument.
For whilst to th' shame of slow-endeavouring art,
10   Thy easie numbers flow, and that each heart
Hath from the leaves of thy unvalu'd Book,
Those Delphick lines with deep impression took,
Then thou our fancy of it self bereaving,
Dost make us Marble with too much conceaving;
And so Sepulcher'd in such pomp dost lie,
That Kings for such a Tomb would wish to die.

1630

L'Allegro

HENCE loathed Melancholy
    Of *Cerberus,* and blackest midnight born,
In *Stygian* Cave forlorn
    'Mongst horrid shapes, and shreiks, and sights unholy,
Find out som uncouth cell,
    Wher brooding darknes spreads his jealous wings,
And the night-Raven sings;
    There under *Ebon* shades, and low-brow'd Rocks,
As ragged as thy Locks,
10   In dark *Cimmerian* desert ever dwell.

But com thou Goddes fair and free,
In Heav'n ycleap'd *Euphrosyne,*
And by men, heart-easing Mirth,
Whom lovely *Venus* at a birth
With two sister Graces more
To Ivy-crowned *Bacchus* bore;
Or whether (as som Sager sing)
The frolick Wind that breathes the Spring,

10 **numbers** verses 11 **unvalu'd** invaluable 12 **Delphick** inspired
as by Apollo, god of music and poetry, who uttered oracles at
Delphi **L'Allegro** Italian, the cheerful man 2 **Cerberus** dog
guarding the entrance to the Greek Hades, the name meaning
"heart-devouring" 3 **Stygian** of the Styx, river in Hades 5 **un-
couth** unknown, desolate 8 **Ebon** black 10 **Cimmerian** gloomy,
the Cimmerii being a people fabled by the ancients to live in a
perpetually dark land in the west 12 **ycleap'd** called **Euphrosyne**
Mirth, one of the three Greek Graces, daughters of Venus, god-
dess of love, and Bacchus, god of wine

Zephir with *Aurora* playing,
As he met her once a Maying,   20
There on Beds of Violets blew,
And fresh-blown Roses washt in dew,
Fill'd her with thee a daughter fair,
So bucksom, blith, and debonair.
Haste thee nymph, and bring with thee
Jest and youthful Jollity,
Quips and Cranks, and wanton Wiles,
Nods, and Becks, and Wreathed Smiles,
Such as hang on *Hebe*'s cheek,
And love to live in dimple sleek;   30
Sport that wrincled Care derides,
And Laughter holding both his sides.
Com, and trip it as ye go
On the light fantastick toe,
And in thy right hand lead with thee,
The Mountain Nymph, sweet Liberty;
And if I give thee honour due,
Mirth, admit me of thy crue
To live with her, and live with thee,
In unreproved pleasures free;   40
To hear the Lark begin his flight,
And singing startle the dull night,
From his watch-towre in the skies,
Till the dappled dawn doth rise;
Then to com in spight of sorrow,
And at my window bid good morrow,
Through the Sweet-Briar, or the Vine,
Or the twisted Eglantine.
While the Cock with lively din,
Scatters the rear of darknes thin,   50
And to the stack, or the Barn dore,
Stoutly struts his Dames before,
Oft list'ning how the Hounds and horn,
Chearly rouse the slumbring morn,

19 **Zephir** spring west wind **Aurora** goddess of dawn 20 **a May-ing** celebrating the spring festival of May 1 when blossoms were gathered 24 **bucksom** lively **debonair** pleasant 27 **Quips** smart sayings **Cranks** oddly humorous turns of speech **wanton wiles** light-hearted tricks 28 **Becks** bows 29 **Hebe** goddess of youth and spring 34 **fantastick** whimsical 40 **unreproved** unreprovable, innocent 45 **in spight of** in order to thwart

From the side of som Hoar Hill,
Through the high wood echoing shrill.
Som time walking not unseen
By Hedge-row Elms, on Hillocks green,
Right against the Eastern gate,
60   Wher the great Sun begins his state,
Rob'd in flames, and Amber light,
The clouds in thousand Liveries dight,
While the Plowman neer at hand,
Whistles ore the Furrow'd Land,
And the Milkmaid singeth blithe,
And the Mower whets his sithe,
And every Shepherd tells his tale
Under the Hawthorn in the dale.
Streit mine eye hath caught new pleasures
70   Whilst the Lantskip round it measures,
Russet Lawns, and Fallows Gray,
Where the nibling flocks do stray,
Mountains on whose barren brest
The labouring clouds do often rest:
Meadows trim with Daisies pide,
Shallow Brooks, and Rivers wide.
Towers, and Battlements it sees
Boosom'd high in tufted Trees,
Wher perhaps som beauty lies,
80   The Cynosure of neighbouring eyes.
Hard by, a Cottage chimney smokes,
From betwixt two aged Okes,
Where *Corydon* and *Thyrsis* met,
Are at their savory dinner set
Of Hearbs, and other Country Messes,
Which the neat-handed *Phillis* dresses;
And then in haste her Bowre she leaves,
With *Thestylis* to bind the Sheaves;
Or if the earlier season lead
90   To the tann'd Haycock in the Mead,
Som times with secure delight

55 **hoar** grey 60 **state** stately progress 62 **dight** arrayed 67 **tells his tale** checks the total number of his flock 75 **pide** spotted 80 **Cynosure** focus of attention 83, 86, 88 **Corydon, Thyrsis, Phillis, Thestylis** conventional names for rustics in classical pastoral poetry 85 **Messes** dishes 87 **Bowre** chamber 91 **secure** free from care

The up-land Hamlets will invite,
When the merry Bells ring round,
And the jocond rebecks sound
To many a youth, and many a maid,
Dancing in the Chequer'd shade;
And young and old com forth to play
On a Sunshine Holyday,
Till the live-long day-light fail,
Then to the Spicy Nut-brown Ale,   100
With stories told of many a feat,
How *Faery Mab* the junkets eat,
She was pincht, and pull'd she sed,
And he by Friars Lanthorn led
Tells how the drudging *Goblin* swet,
To ern his Cream-bowle duly set,
When in one night, ere glimps of morn,
His shadowy Flale hath thresh'd the Corn
That ten day-labourers could not end,
Then lies him down the Lubbar Fend.   110
And stretch'd out all the Chimney's length,
Basks at the fire his hairy strength;
And Crop-full out of dores he flings,
Ere the first Cock his Mattin rings.
Thus don the Tales, to bed they creep,
By whispering Windes soon lull'd asleep.
Towred Cities please us then,
And the busie humm of men,
Where throngs of Knights and Barons bold,
In weeds of Peace high triumphs hold,   120
With store of Ladies, whose bright eies
Rain influence, and judge the prise
Of Wit, or Arms, while both contend
To win her Grace, whom all commend.
There let *Hymen* oft appear

94 **jocond rebecks** cheerful fiddles 102 **Mab** queen of fairies
104 **he by** *1645; 1673 reads* "by the" **Friars Lanthorn** jack-o'-
lantern, will-o'-the-wisp 105 **Goblin** Robin Goodfellow, the
lines that follow about him relate to a popular superstition
110 **Lubbar Fend** clumsy fiend or sprite 111 **Chimney** fire-
place 114 **Matin** morning hymn 120 **weeds** garments **triumphs**
celebrations 121 **store** plenty 122 **rain influence** exert such a
power to affect events as stars were thought to possess
125 **Hymen** classical god of marriage

In Saffron robe, with Taper clear,
And pomp, and feast, and revelry,
With mask, and antique Pageantry,
Such sights as youthfull Poets dream
130   On Summer eeves by haunted stream.
Then to the well-trod stage anon,
If *Jonsons* learned Sock be on,
Or sweetest *Shakespear* fancies childe,
Warble his native Wood-notes wilde,
And ever against eating Cares,
Lap me in soft *Lydian* Aires,
Married to immortal verse
Such as the meeting soul may pierce
In notes, with many a winding bout
140   Of lincked sweetnes long drawn out,
With wanton heed, and giddy cunning,
The melting voice through mazes running;
Untwisting all the chains that ty
The hidden soul of harmony.
That *Orpheus* self may heave his head
From golden slumber on a bed
Of heapt *Elysian* flowres, and hear
Such streins as would have won the ear
Of *Pluto,* to have quite set free
150   His half regain'd *Eurydice.*
These delights, if thou canst give,
Mirth with thee, I mean to live.

? 1630-32

128 **mask** masque, a kind of dramatic spectacle 132 **Jonson** Ben Jonson, dramatist contemporary with Shakespeare **Sock** low-heeled shoe worn by actors in classical comedy 136 **Lydian** one of the kinds of Greek music, sweet and soft 139 **bout** involution 141 **wanton** playful 145-50 Orpheus, legendary Greek musican, was allowed to lead back his dead wife Eurydice from Hades because his skill so greatly pleased its god and goddess, Pluto and Proserpine, but he failed to heed the warning not to look back at her on the way out into the light and she was lost to him again 147 **Elysian** Paradisal

ack. of life's melancholy

Il Penseroso

HENCE vain deluding joyes,
 The brood of folly without father bred,
How little you bested,
 Or fill the fixed mind with all your toyes;
Dwell in som idle brain,
 And fancies fond with gaudy shapes possess,
As thick and numberless
 As the gay motes that people the Sun Beams,
Or likest hovering dreams
 The fickle Pensioners of *Morpheus* train.   10

But hail thou Goddes, sage and holy,
Hail divinest Melancholy,
Whose Saintly visage is too bright
To hit the Sense of human sight;
And therfore to our weaker view,
Ore laid with black staid Wisdoms hue.
Black, but such as in esteem,
Prince *Memnons* sister might beseem,
Or that Starr'd *Ethiope* Queen that strove
To set her beauties praise above   20
The Sea Nymphs, and their powers offended.
Yet thou art higher far descended,
Thee bright-hair'd *Vesta* long of yore,
To solitary *Saturn* bore;
His daughter she (in *Saturns* raign,
Such mixture was not held a stain)
Oft in glimmering Bowres, and glades
He met her, and in secret shades
Of woody *Ida*'s inmost grove,
While yet there was no fear of *Jove*.   30

Il Penseroso Italian, the thoughtful or meditative man 3 **bested**
be-stead, help 6 **fond** foolish 10 **Morpheus** god of sleep
18 **Memnon** legendary Ethiopian prince, famous for his hand-
someness 19 **Ethiope Queen** Cassiopea who, according to a leg-
end here modified, was turned into a star for boastng of her
daughter's beauty 23 **Vesta** goddess of purity 24-30 **Saturn**
father of the gods, reigned on Mount Ida in Crete until deposed
by his son Jove

Com pensive Nun, devout and pure,
Sober, stedfast, and demure,
All in a robe of darkest grain,
Flowing with majestick train,
And sable stole of *Cipres* Lawn,
Over thy decent shoulders drawn.
Com, but keep thy wonted state,
With eev'n step, and musing gate,
And looks commercing with the skies,
40 Thy rapt soul sitting in thine eyes:
There held in holy passion still,
Forget thy self to Marble, till
With a sad Leaden downward cast,
Thou fix them on the earth as fast.
And joyn with thee calm Peace, and Quiet,
Spare Fast, that oft with gods doth diet,
And hears the Muses in a ring,
Ay round about *Joves* Altar sing.
And adde to these retired leasure,
50 That in trim Gardens takes his pleasure;
But first, and chiefest, with thee bring,
Him that yon soars on golden wing,
Guiding the fiery-wheeled throne,
The Cherub Contemplation,
And the mute Silence hist along,
'Less *Philomel* will daign a Song,
In her sweetest, saddest plight,
Smoothing the rugged brow of night,
While *Cynthia* checks her Dragon yoke,
60 Gently o're th'accustom'd Oke;
Sweet Bird that shunn'st the noise of folly,
Most musicall, most melancholy!
Thee Chauntress oft the Woods among,
I woo to hear thy eeven-Song;
And missing thee, I walk unseen
On the dry smooth-shaven Green,

33 **grain** hue 35 **Cipres lawn** black crape 36 **decent** comely
37 **wonted state** habitual dignity 39 **commercing** communing
52-4 Ezekiel x 54 **Cherub Contemplation** contemplation or
knowledge of divine things being the chief faculty of the Cher-
ubim, one of the nine orders of angels 56 **Philomel** nightingale
59 **Cynthia** moon goddess

To behold the wandring Moon,
Riding neer her highest noon,
Like one that had bin led astray
Through the Heav'ns wide pathles way;   70
And oft, as if her head she bow'd,
Stooping through a fleecy cloud.
Oft on a Plat of rising ground,
I hear the far-off *Curfeu* sound,
Over som wide-water'd shoar,
Swinging slow with sullen roar;
Or if the Ayr will not permit,
Som still removed place will fit,
Where glowing Embers through the room
Teach light to counterfeit a gloom,   80
Far from all resort of mirth,
Save the Cricket on the hearth,
Or the Belmans drousie charm,
To bless the dores from nightly harm:
Or let my Lamp at midnight hour,
Be seen in som high lonely Towr,
Where I may oft out-watch the *Bear*,
With thrice great *Hermes,* or unsphear
The spirit of *Plato* to unfold
What Worlds, or what vast Regions hold   90
The immortal mind that hath forsook
Her mansion in this fleshly nook:
And of those *Dæmons* that are found
In fire, air, flood, or under ground,
Whose power hath a true consent
With Planet, or with Element.
Som time let Gorgeous Tragedy
In Scepter'd Pall com sweeping by,

83 **Belman** watchman **charm** chant, marking the hours 87 **Bear** constellation Great Bear or Dipper, visible all night 88 **Hermes** Hermes Trismegistus, seer of Greek and Egyptian legend possessing mystical insight **unsphear** call down from the celestial sphere it inhabits 89-96 The use of symbol and myth for purposes of exposition in the writings of the Greek philosopher, Plato, made them a chief source of classical and mediaeval ideas about the soul's future and about spiritual beings or demons and the mysterious powers they were thought to exercise through material things like the planets and elements 95 **consent** agreement 98 **Pall** mantle

Presenting *Thebs,* or *Pelops* line,
100   Or the tale of *Troy* divine.
Or what (though rare) of later age,
Ennobled hath the Buskind stage.
But, O sad virgin, that thy power
Might raise *Musæus* from his bower,
Or bid the soul of *Orpheus* sing
Such notes as warbled to the string,
Drew Iron tears down *Pluto*'s cheek,
And made Hell grant what Love did seek.
Or call up him that left half told
110   The story of *Cambuscan* bold,
Of *Camball,* and of *Algarsife,*
And who had *Canace* to wife,
That own'd the vertuous Ring and Glass,
And of the wondrous Hors of Brass,
On which the *Tartar* King did ride;
And if ought els, great *Bards* beside,
In sage and solemn tunes have sung,
Of Turneys and of Trophies hung;
Of Forests, and inchantments drear,
120   Where more is meant then meets the ear.
Thus night oft see me in thy pale career,
Till civil-suited Morn appeer,
Not trickt and frounc't as she was wont,

99-100 Stories of the city of Thebes (and its ruler Oedipus), of the descendants of Pelops (as Agamemnon, Orestes, Iphigenia, Electra), and of the consequences of the Trojan war, provide the plots for Greek tragedy as written by Sophocles, Aeschylus, Euripides 102 **Buskin** high-heeled shoe worn by Greek actors in tragedy 104 **Musaeus** legendary Greek poet 105 **Orpheus** see "L'Allegro," 145-50 109-15 The unfinished "Squire's Tale" in *The Canterbury Tales* of the fourteenth-century English poet Geoffrey Chaucer is an oriental story of chivalry and wonders concerning the Tartar king Cambuscan (Gengis Khan), his sons and daughter, involving a ring of magical virtue or power which enabled the wearer to understand the language of birds and the healing qualities of herbs, a mirror which foretold disasters, and a flying horse of brass 116-20 The romances of chivalry written by the sixteenth-century Italian poets Ariosto and Tasso, and in particular *The Faerie Queene* of the Elizabethan poet Edmund Spenser, who was much admired by Milton, use knightly adventure for purposes of moral allegory 122 **civil-suited** soberly clad 123 **trickt** decked **frounc't** with curled hair

With the Attick Boy to hunt,
But Cherchef't in a comly Cloud,
While rocking Winds are Piping loud,
Or usher'd with a shower still,
When the gust hath blown his fill,
Ending on the russling Leaves,
With minute drops from off the Eaves.   130
And when the Sun begins to fling
His flaring beams, me Goddes bring
To arched walks of twilight groves,
And shadows brown that *Sylvan* loves
Of Pine, or monumental Oake,
Where the rude Ax with heaved stroke,
Was never heard the Nymphs to daunt,
Or fright them from their hallow'd haunt.
There in close covert by som Brook,
Where no profaner eye may look,   140
Hide me from Day's garish eie,
While the Bee with Honied thie,
That at her flowry work doth sing,
And the Waters murmuring
With such consort as they keep,
Entice the dewy-feather'd Sleep;
And let som strange mysterious dream,
Wave at his Wings in Airy stream,
Of lively portrature display'd,
Softly on my eye-lids laid.   150
And as I wake, sweet musick breath
Above, about, or underneath,
Sent by som spirit to mortals good,
Or th'unseen Genius of the Wood.
But let my due feet never fail,
To walk the studious Cloysters pale,
And love the high embowed Roof,
With antick Pillars massy proof,
And storied Windows richly dight,
Casting a dimm religious light.   160
There let the pealing Organ blow,

124 **Attic boy** Cephalus, beloved by Aurora, dawn goddess
134 **Sylvan** god of forests 137 **Nymphs** tree deities 145 **consort** harmony 154 **Genius** local divinity 156 **pale** enclosure
157 **embowed** arched 158 **antick** quaintly ornamented **proof** solid 159 **dight** decorated

*as a result
of melancholy
we can
appreciate
joys*

To the full voic'd Quire below,
In Service high, and Anthems cleer,
As may with sweetnes, through mine ear,
Dissolve me into extasies,
And bring all Heav'n before mine eyes.
And may at last my weary age
Find out the peacefull hermitage,
The Hairy Gown and Mossy Cell,
170 Where I may sit and rightly spell,
Of every Star that Heav'n doth shew,
And every Herb that sips the dew;
Till old experience do attain
To something like Prophetic strain.
These pleasures *Melancholy* give,
And I with thee will choose to live.

? 1630-32

Song: On May Morning

Now the bright morning Star, Dayes harbinger,
Comes dancing from the East, and leads with her
The Flowry *May*, who from her green lap throws
The yellow Cowslip, and the pale Primrose.
  Hail Bounteous *May* that dost inspire
  Mirth and youth, and warm desire,
  Woods and Groves, are of thy dressing,
  Hill and Dale, doth boast thy blessing.
Thus we salute thee with our early Song,
10   And welcom thee, and wish thee long.

? 1629

At a Solemn Musick

BLEST pair of *Sirens*, pledges of Heav'ns joy,
Sphear-born harmonious Sisters, Voice, and Vers,
Wed your divine sounds, and mixt power employ
Dead things with inbreath'd sense able to pierce,
And to our high-rais'd phantasie present,

170 **spell** ponder 1 **Sirens** celestial beings. In his account of the
Myth of Er (*Republic*, X, 616-17) Plato wrote that a siren dwells
upon each of the astronomical spheres (see "Christ's Nativity,"
125) singing its musical note. 5 **phantasie** imagination

That undisturbed Song of pure concent,
Ay sung before the saphire-colour'd throne
To him that sits theron
With Saintly shout, and solemn Jubily,
Where the bright Seraphim in burning row   10
Their loud up-lifted Angel trumpets blow,
And the Cherubick host in thousand quires
Touch their immortal Harps of golden wires,
With those just Spirits that wear victorious Palms,
Hymns devout and holy Psalms
Singing everlastingly;
That we on Earth with undiscording voice
May rightly answer that melodious noise;
As once we did, till disproportion'd sin
Jarr'd against natures chime, and with harsh din   20
Broke the fair musick that all creatures made
To their great Lord, whose love their motion sway'd
In perfect Diapason, whilst they stood
In first obedience, and their state of good.
O may we soon again renew that Song,
And keep in tune with Heav'n, till God ere long
To his celestial consort us unite,
To live with him, and sing in endles morn of light.

                                        P 1632-3

Lycidas

In this Monody the Author bewails a learned Friend, unfortunatly drown'd in his Passage from *Chester* on the *Irish* Seas, 1637. And by occasion foretels the ruine of our corrupted Clergy then in their height.

YET once more, O ye Laurels, and once more
Ye Myrtles brown, with Ivy never-sear,
I com to pluck your Berries harsh and crude,
And with forc'd fingers rude,
Shatter your leaves before the mellowing year.
Bitter constraint, and sad occasion dear,
Compels me to disturb your season due:

6 **concent** harmony; *1673*, "concent"; *1645*, "content" 7 Ezekiel 1.26 9 **Jubily** rejoicing for salvation 12-16 Revelation XIV 23 **Diapason** concord 27 **consort** group of musicians 1-2 **Laurels, Myrtles, Ivy** symbols of immortality and poetry 2 **sere** withered 3 **crude** unripe

For *Lycidas* is dead, dead ere his prime
Young *Lycidas*, and hath not left his peer:
10 Who would not sing for *Lycidas?* he knew
Himself to sing, and build the lofty rhyme.
He must not flote upon his watry bear
Unwept, and welter to the parching wind,
Without the meed of som melodious tear.
    Begin then, Sisters of the sacred well,
That from beneath the seat of *Jove* doth spring,
Begin, and somewhat loudly sweep the string.
Hence with denial vain, and coy excuse,
So may som gentle Muse
20 With lucky words favour my destin'd Urn,
And as he passes turn,
And bid fair peace be to my sable shrowd.
For we were nurst upon the self-same hill,
Fed the same flock; by fountain, shade, and rill.
    Together both, ere the high Lawns appear'd
Under the opening eye-lids of the morn,
We drove a field, and both together heard
What time the Gray-fly winds her sultry horn,
Batt'ning our flocks with the fresh dews of night,
30 Oft till the Star that rose, at Ev'ning, bright
Toward Heav'ns descent had slop'd his westering wheel.
Mean while the Rural ditties were not mute,
Temper'd to th'Oaten Flute,
Rough *Satyrs* danc'd, and *Fauns* with clov'n heel,
From the glad sound would not be absent long,
And old *Damœtas* lov'd to hear our song.
    But O the heavy change, now thou art gon,
Now thou art gon, and never must return!
Thee Shepherd, thee the Woods, and desert Caves,

8 **Lycidas** a conventional name in pastoral poetry, here standing
for Edward King who was at Christ's College, Cambridge, with
Milton, had written Latin poems and looked forward to a career
as a clergyman 9 **peer** equal 13 **welter** toss 14 **meed** tribute
15 **Sisters . . . well** the nine Muses, born beside the Pierian
spring on Mount Olympus where Jove had his throne 18 **coy**
modest 20 **lucky** propitious 25 **high lawns** upland meadows
28 **winds** blows **sultry** in the noon heat 29 **batt'ning** fattening
33 **temper'd** attuned **Oaten** reed 34 **Satyrs, Fauns** country di-
vinities, half man, half goat 36 **Damoetas** conventional pastoral
name, perhaps here indicating Joseph Mede, an admired tutor
of Christ's College

With wilde Thyme and the gadding Vine o'regrown,   40
And all their echoes mourn.
The Willows, and the Hazle Copses green,
Shall now no more be seen,
Fanning their joyous Leaves to thy soft layes.
As killing as the Canker to the Rose,
Or Taint-worm to the weanling Herds that graze,
Or Frost to Flowers, that their gay wardrop wear,
When first the White thorn blows;
Such, *Lycidas*, thy loss to Shepherds ear.
　　Where were ye Nymphs when the remorseless deep   50
Clos'd o're the head of your lov'd *Lycidas*?
For neither were ye playing on the steep,
Where your old *Bards*, the famous *Druids* ly,
Nor on the shaggy top of *Mona* high,
Nor yet where *Deva* spreads her wisard stream:
Aye me, I fondly dream!
Had ye bin there—for what could that have don?
What could the Muse her self that *Orpheus* bore,
The Muse her self, for her inchanting son
Whom Universal nature did lament,   60
When by the rout that made the hideous roar,
His goary visage down the stream was sent,
Down the swift *Hebrus* to the *Lesbian* shore.
　　Alas! What boots it with uncessant care
To tend the homely slighted Shepherds trade,
And strictly meditate the thankles Muse,
Were it not better don as others use,
To sport with *Amaryllis* in the shade,

40 **gadding** straggling 48 **blows** blooms 50 **Nymphs** deities of
woods and fields 52 **steep** mountain 53 **Druids** ancient British
or Welsh priests and poets, thought to be buried on a mountain
in Wales overlooking the Irish Sea 54 **Mona** isle of Anglesey in
the Irish Sea, an ancient center of Druidism 55 **Deva** river
Dee **wisard** because the shifting of its course was thought to
foretell good or evil for England on one bank or Wales on the
other 56 **fondly** foolishly 58 **Muse** Calliope, muse of epic
poetry 61-3 **Orpheus,** legendary poet and musician, was torn
limb from limb by a howling mob of Thracian women, devotees
of Bacchus, god of wine, when they found him enchanting rocks
and trees with his song. His head floated down the river Hebrus
and across the Aegean sea to the island of Lesbos where it was
buried. 64 **boots** profits 68, 69 **Amaryllis, Neaera** conventional
pastoral names for nymphs

Or with the tangles of *Neæra's* hair?
70 *Fame* is the spur that the clear spirit doth raise
    (That last infirmity of Noble mind)
    To scorn delights, and live laborious dayes;
    But the fair Guerdon when we hope to find,
    And think to burst out into sudden blaze,
    Comes the blind *Fury* with th'abhorred shears,
    And slits the thin-spun life. But not the praise,
    Phœbus repli'd, and touch'd my trembling ears;
    Fame is no plant that grows on mortal soil,
    Nor in the glistering foil
80 Set off to th'world, nor in broad rumour lies,
    But lives and spreds aloft by those pure eyes,
    And perfet witnes of all judging *Jove;*
    As he pronounces lastly on each deed,
    Of so much fame in Heav'n expect thy meed.
        O Fountain *Arethuse,* and thou honour'd floud,
    Smooth-sliding *Mincius,* crown'd with vocall reeds,
    That strain I heard was of a higher mood:
    But now my Oat proceeds,
    And listens to the Herald of the Sea
90 That came in *Neptune's* plea,
    He ask'd the Waves, and ask'd the Fellon winds,
    What hard mishap hath doom'd this gentle swain?
    And question'd every gust of rugged wings
    That blows from off each beaked Promontory,
    They knew not of his story,
    And sage *Hippotades* their answer brings,
    That not a blast was from his dungeon stray'd,
    The Ayr was calm, and on the level brine,
    Sleek *Panope* with all her sisters play'd.
100 It was that fatall and perfidious Bark
    Built in th'eclipse, and rigg'd with curses dark,

73 **Guerdon** reward 75 **Fury** Atropos, one of the Fates of classical myth 77 **Phoebus** Apollo, god of poetry and sun 79 **foil** setting for a gem 85 **Arethuse** Sicilian fountain. Both Arethusa and Alpheus (below, line 132) are regularly invoked as muses by the classical pastoral poets 86 **Mincius** river of Lombardy described by Virgil in his pastoral *Eclogues* 88 **Oat** shepherds reed-pipe or flute 89 **Herald of the Sea** Triton, Neptune's messenger 90 **plea** defence 96 **Hippotades** god of winds 99 **Panope** chief of the nereids or sea nymphs 100 **bark** ship

That sunk so low that sacred head of thine.
 Next *Camus,* reverend Sire, went footing slow,
His Mantle hairy, and his Bonnet sedge,
Inwrought with figures dim, and on the edge
Like to that sanguine flower inscrib'd with woe.
Ah! Who hath reft (quoth he) my dearest pledge?
Last came, and last did go,
The Pilot of the *Galilean* lake,
Two massy Keyes he bore of metals twain,   110
(The Golden opes, the Iron shuts amain)
He shook his Miter'd locks, and stern bespake,
How well could I have spar'd for thee young swain,
Anow of such as for their bellies sake,
Creep and intrude, and climb into the fold?
Of other care they little reck'ning make,
Then how to scramble at the shearers feast,
And shove away the worthy bidden guest.
Blind mouthes! that scarce themselves know how to hold
A Sheep-hook, or have learn'd ought els the least   120
That to the faithfull Herdmans art belongs!
What recks it them? What need they? They are sped;
And when they list, their lean and flashy songs
Grate on their scrannel Pipes of wretched straw,
The hungry Sheep look up, and are not fed,
But swoln with wind, and the rank mist they draw,
Rot inwardly, and foul contagion spread:
Besides what the grim Woolf with privy paw
Daily devours apace, and nothing sed,
But that two-handed engine at the door,   130
Stands ready to smite once, and smite no more.
 Return *Alpheus,* the dread voice is past,
That shrunk thy streams; Return *Sicilian* Muse,
And call the Vales, and bid them hither cast

103 **Camus** river Cam, representing Cambridge University
106 **sanguine flower** purple-streaked hyacinth, according to
Greek story sprung from and marked by the blood of Hyacin-
thus, a youth loved and accidentally slain by Apollo 107 **pledge**
promising child 109 **Pilot** St. Peter 110 Matthew XVI: 19
111 **amain** with force 122 **What . . . them?** What do they care?
are sped have prospered 123 **list** are inclined 124 **scrannel** harsh,
or perhaps feeble 126 **draw** breathe 128 **Woolf** Antichrist or
Satan, John x:1 **privy** hidden 130 **two-handed engine** an instru-
ment of divine retribution, perhaps the sword of Justice or of
Michael, the avenging angel 132 **Alpheus** Arcadian river

Their Bels, and Flourets of a thousand hues.
Ye valleys low where the milde whispers use,
Of shades and wanton winds, and gushing brooks,
On whose fresh lap the swart Star sparely looks,
Throw hither all your quaint enameld eyes,
140 That on the green terf suck the honied showres,
And purple all the ground with vernal flowres.
Bring the rathe Primrose that forsaken dies,
The tufted Crow-toe, and pale Gessamine,
The white Pink, and the Pansie freakt with jeat,
The glowing Violet,
The Musk-rose, and the well attir'd Woodbine,
With Cowslips wan that hang the pensive hed,
And every flower that sad embroidery wears:
Bid *Amaranthus* all his beauty shed,
150 And Daffadillies fill their cups with tears,
To strew the Laureat Herse where *Lycid* lies.
For so to interpose a little ease,
Let our frail thoughts dally with false surmise.
Ay me! Whilst thee the shores, and sounding Seas
Wash far away, where ere thy bones are hurld,
Whether beyond the stormy *Hebrides,*
Where thou perhaps under the whelming tide
Visit'st the bottom of the monstrous world;
Or whether thou to our moist vows deny'd,
160 Sleep'st by the fable of *Bellerus* old,
Where the great vision of the guarded Mount
Looks toward *Namancos* and *Bayona's* hold;
Look homeward Angel now, and melt with ruth.
And, O ye *Dolphins,* waft the haples youth.

  Weep no more, woful Shepherds weep no more,
For *Lycidas* your sorrow is not dead,

136 **use** haunt 138 **swart** heat-darkened **Star** Dog-star, Sirius
whose influence was associated with late-summer heat 142 **rathe**
early 144 **freak't** spotted 149 **Amaranthus** Greek unfading,
type of immortality 156 **Hebrides** islands off the west coast of
Scotland 160 **Bellerus** giant of Land's End, western tip of Corn-
wall, a district prominent in British legend 161 St. Michael's
Mount, off Cornwall, guarded the western coast and was guarded
by the angel Michael who was said to have appeared in visions
there. 162 **Namancos, Bayona's hold** district and stronghold on
the coast of Spain 163 **ruth** pity 164 **Dolphins** sea-creatures,
much affected by music, who saved the lyric poet Arion of Les-
bos when he was cast into the sea by sailors

Sunk though he be beneath the watry floar,
So sinks the day-star in the Ocean bed,
And yet anon repairs his drooping head,
And tricks his beams, and with new spangled Ore,   170
Flames in the forehead of the morning sky:
So *Lycidas* sunk low, but mounted high,
Through the dear might of him that walk'd the waves
Where other groves, and other streams along,
With *Nectar* pure his oozy Lock's he laves,
And hears the unexpressive nuptiall Song,
In the blest Kingdoms meek of joy and love.
There entertain him all the Saints above,
In solemn troops, and sweet Societies
That sing, and singing in their glory move,   180
And wipe the tears for ever from his eyes.
Now *Lycidas* the Shepherds weep no more;
Hence forth thou art the Genius of the shore,
In thy large recompense, and shalt be good
To all that wander in that perilous flood.

  Thus sang the uncouth Swain to th'Okes and rills,
While the still morn went out with Sandals gray,
He touch'd the tender stops of various Quills,
With eager thought warbling his *Dorick* lay:
And now the Sun had stretch'd out all the hills,   190
And now was dropt into the Western bay;
At last he rose, and twitch'd his Mantle blew:
To morrow to fresh Woods, and Pastures new.

1637

168 **day-star** sun 170 **tricks** beautifies **Ore** gold 173 **him** Christ,
Matthew xiv: 25 176-81 Revelation xix: 6-7, xiv: 1-5, vii: 17,
xxi: 4 176 **unexpressive** inexpressible 183 **Genius** local deity
186 **uncouth** unknown 188 **Quills** reed-pipes 189 **Doric** because
the Greek pastoral poets, Theocritus, Bion, Moschus, used the
Doric dialect 192 **twitch'd** threw on

SONNETS

O NIGHTINGALE

O Nightingale, that on yon bloomy Spray
  Warbl'st at eeve, when all the Woods are still,
  Thou with fresh hope the Lovers heart dost fill,
  While the jolly hours lead on propitious *May*,
Thy liquid notes that close the eye of Day,
  First heard before the shallow Cuccoo's bill
  Portend success in love; O if *Jove*'s will
  Have linkt that amorous power to thy soft lay,
Now timely sing, ere the rude Bird of Hate
10   Foretell my hopeles doom in som Grove ny:
  As thou from yeer to yeer hast sung too late
For my relief; yet hadst no reason why,
  Whether the Muse, or Love call thee his mate,
  Both them I serve, and of their train am I.

? 1629

HOW SOON HATH TIME

How soon hath Time the suttle theef of youth,
  Stoln on his wing my three and twentieth yeer!
  My hasting dayes flie on with full career,
  But my late spring no bud or blossom shew'th.
Perhaps my semblance might deceive the truth,
20   That I to manhood am arriv'd so near,
  And inward ripenes doth much less appear,
  That some more timely-happy spirits indu'th.
Yet be it less or more, or soon or slow,
  It shall be still in strictest measure eev'n,
  To that same lot, however mean, or high,
Toward which Time leads me, and the will of Heav'n;
  All is, if I have grace to use it so,
  As ever in my great task Masters eye.

1632

28

ON THE DETRACTION WHICH FOLLOW'D UPON MY WRITING CERTAIN TREATISES

I did but prompt the age to quit their cloggs
   By the known rules of antient libertie,
   When strait a barbarous noise environs me
Of Owles and Cuckoos, Asses, Apes and Doggs.
As when those Hinds that were transform'd to Froggs
   Raild at *Latona's* twin-born progenie
   Which after held the Sun and Moon in fee.
But this is got by casting Pearl to Hoggs;
That bawle for freedom in their senceless mood,
   And still revolt when truth would set them free.   10
   Licence they mean when they cry libertie;
For who loves that, must first be wise and good;
   But from that mark how far they roave we see
   For all this wast of wealth, and loss of blood.

                            ? 1646

ON THE LORD GEN. FAIRFAX AT THE SEIGE OF COLCHESTER

Fairfax, whose name in armes through Europe rings
   Filling each mouth with envy, or with praise,
   And all her jealous monarchs with amaze,
   And rumors loud, that daunt remotest kings,
Thy firm unshak'n vertue ever brings
   Victory home, though new rebellions raise   20

On . . . **Treatises** title from Trinity College Manuscript; text
1673. The treatises on divorce, published in 1643, 1644, 1645,
had brought Milton into disrepute with the strict Puritans.
5-7 With her children Apollo and Diana, afterwards deities of
sun and moon, Latona was driven out of Olympus by Jove's
jealous wife Juno, and was mocked in her wanderings by peas-
ants whom Jove turned into frogs. **7 in fee** in absolute posses-
sion 8 Matthew VII: **6**

On . , . **Colchester** text of this and the two following sonnets
from the Trinity College Manuscript. Sir Thomas Fairfax, gen-
eral of the parliamentary armies in the Civil War, besieged the
Scots at Colchester in 1648, after their defection from the par-

Thir Hydra heads, & the fals North displaies
Her brok'n league, to impe their serpent wings,
O yet a nobler task awaites thy hand;
    For what can Warr, but endless warr still breed,
    Till Truth, & Right from Violence be freed,
And Public Faith cleard from the shamefull brand
    Of Public Fraud. In vain doth Valour bleed
    While Avarice, & Rapine share the land.

1648

TO THE LORD GENERALL CROMWELL

May, 1652

On the proposalls of certaine ministers at the Committee for
Propagation of the Gospell.

Cromwell, our cheif of men, who through a cloud
10   Not of warr onely, but detractions rude,
    Guided by faith & matchless Fortitude
    To peace & truth thy glorious way hast plough'd,
And on the neck of crowned Fortune proud
    Has reard Gods Trophies, & his work pursu'd,
    While Darwen stream with blood of Scotts imbru'd,
    And Dunbarr feild resounds thy praises loud,
And Worsters laureat wreath; yet much remaines
    To conquer still; peace hath her victories
    No less renownd then warr, new foes aries
20   Threatning to bind our soules with secular chaines:
    Helpe us to save free Conscience from the paw
    Of hireling wolves whose Gospell is their maw.

1652

liamentary cause. 1 **Hydra** many-headed serpent slain by Her-
cules 2 **league** the Solemn League and Covenant of 1643
between English and Scots
To . . . Gospell Cromwell succeeded Fairfax as general. The
Parliamentary Committee had proposed that preachers be su-
pervised and paid by parliamentary authority 15-17 Battles in
which Cromwell defeated the Scots between 1648 and 1651
20 secular chaines civil laws restraining religion 22 **maw** stomach

TO SR. HENRY VANE THE YOUNGER

Vane, young in yeares, but in sage counsell old,
   Then whome a better Senatour nere held
   The helme of Rome, when gownes not armes repelld
   The feirce Epeirot & the African bold,
Whether to settle peace or to unfold
   The drift of hollow states hard to be spelld,
   Then to advise how warr may best, upheld,
   Move by her two maine nerves, Iron & Gold
In all her equipage; besides to know
   Both spirituall powre & civill, what each meanes   10
   What severs each thou 'hast learnt, which few have don.
The bounds of either sword to thee wee ow.
   Therfore on thy firme hand religion leanes
   In peace, & reck'ns thee her eldest son.

1652

ON THE LATE MASSACHER IN PIEMONT

Avenge O Lord thy slaughter'd Saints, whose bones
   Lie scatter'd on the Alpine mountains cold,
   Ev'n them who kept thy truth so pure of old
   When all our Fathers worship't Stocks and Stones,
Forget not: in thy book record their groanes
   Who were thy Sheep and in their antient Fold   20
   Slayn by the bloody *Piemontese* that roll'd
   Mother with Infant down the Rocks. Their moans
The Vales redoubl'd to the Hills, and they
   To Heav'n. Their martyr'd blood and ashes sow
   O're all th'*Italian* fields where still doth sway
The triple Tyrant: that from these may grow
   A hunder'd-fold, who having learnt thy way
   Early may fly the *Babylonian* wo.

1655

1 **Vane,** a leader in the Long Parliament 4 **Epeirot** Pyrrhus of
Epirus **African** Hannibal 8 **nerves** sinews
On . . . Piemont text from 1673. The Waldensian Protestants of
Piedmont, declared heretics in the thirteenth century, were mas-
sacred in 1655 26 **triple Tyrant,** the Pope, alluding to the triple
mitre 28 **Babylonian Revelation** xvii-xviii

WHEN I CONSIDER

When I consider how my light is spent,
   E're half my days, in this dark world and wide,
   And that one Talent which is death to hide,
   Lodg'd with me useless, though my Soul more bent
To serve therewith my Maker, and present
   My true account, least he returning chide,
   Doth God exact day-labour, light deny'd,
   I fondly ask; But patience to prevent
That murmur, soon replies, God doth not need
10   Either man's work or his own gifts, who best
   Bear his milde yoak, they serve him best, his State
Is Kingly. Thousands at his bidding speed
   And post o're Land and Ocean without rest:
   They also serve who only stand and waite.

One serves by having faith   *P 1652*
use blindness to serve God

LAWRENCE

Lawrence of vertuous Father vertuous Son,
   Now that the Fields are dank, and ways are mire,
   Where shall we sometimes meet, and by the fire
   Help wast a sullen day; what may be won
From the hard Season gaining: time will run
20   On smoother, till *Favonius* re-inspire
   The frozen earth; and cloth in fresh attire
   The Lillie and Rose, that neither sow'd nor spun.
What neat repast shall feast us, light and choice,
   Of Attick tast, with Wine, whence we may rise
   To hear the Lute well toucht, or artfull voice
Warble immortal Notes and *Tuskan* Ayre?
   He who of those delights can judge, And spare
   To interpose them oft, is not unwise.

1655

1 **When I consider** . . . and 15 **Lawrence** . . . text from 1673
1 Milton became totally blind early in 1652 3 Matthew **xxv**
8 **fondly** foolishly 12 **Thousands** of angels 14 **They** the higher
orders of angels who surround God's throne and serve him by
love, knowledge, contemplation
15 **Lawrence** Edward, son of the Lord President of the Council
under Cromwell 18 **wast** spend 20 **Favonius** spring west wind;
see Horace *Odes,* I, iv 22 Matthew **vi**: 28

TO MR. CYRIACK SKINNER UPON HIS
BLINDNESS

Cyriack, this three years day these eys, though clear
 To outward view, of blemish or of spot;
 Bereft of light thir seeing have forgot,
 Nor to thir idle orbs doth sight appear
Of Sun or Moon or Starre throughout the year,
 Or man or woman. Yet I argue not
 Against heavns hand or will, nor bate a jot
 Of heart or hope; but still bear vp and steer
Right onward. What supports me, dost thou ask?
 The conscience, Friend, to have lost them overply'd 10
 In libertyes defence, my noble task,
Of which all Europe talks from side to side.
 This thought might lead me through the world's vain
  mask
 Content though blind, had I no better guide.

            1655

METHOUGHT I SAW

Methought I saw my late espoused Saint
 Brought to me like *Alcestis* from the grave,
 Whom *Joves* great Son to her glad Husband gave,
 Rescu'd from death by force though pale and faint.
Mine as whom washt from spot of child-bed taint, 20
 Purification in the old Law did save,
 And such, as yet once more I trust to have
 Full sight of her in Heaven without restraint,
Came vested all in white, pure as her mind:
 Her face was vail'd, yet to my fancied sight,
 Love, sweetness, goodness, in her person shin'd
So clear, as in no face with more delight.
 But O as to embrace me she enclin'd
 I wak'd, she fled, and day brought back my night.
            ? 1658

To . . . Blindness text from the Trinity College Manuscript. Skinner had been one of Milton's pupils 15-28 text from 1673. Milton's second wife, Katherine Woodcock, died in childbirth in 1658, fifteen months after their marriage. 16 **Alcestis** died for her husband Admetus, but was brought back veiled from Hades by Hercules, Jove's son 19-20 Leviticus XII

ON THE NEW FORCERS OF CONSCIENCE
UNDER THE LONG PARLIAMENT

Because you have thrown of your Prelate Lord,
    And with stiff Vowes renounc'd his Liturgie
    To seise the widdow'd whore Pluralitie
From them whose sin ye envi'd, not abhor'd,
Dare ye for this adjure the Civill Sword
    To force our Consciences that Christ set free,
    And ride us with a classic Hierarchy
Taught ye by meer *A. S.* and *Rotherford?*
Men whose Life, Learning, Faith and pure intent
10   Would have been held in high esteem with *Paul*
    Must now be nam'd and printed Hereticks
By shallow *Edwards* and Scotch what d'ye call:
    But we do hope to find out all your tricks,
    Your plots and packing wors then those of *Trent,*
              That so the Parliament
May with their wholsom and preventive Shears
Clip your Phylacteries, though bauk your Ears,
            And succour our just Fears
When they shall read this clearly in your charge
New Presbyter is but *Old Priest* writ Large.

P 1646

On . . . Parliament text from 1673. The poem, a sonnetto caudata or sonnet with coda or tail, deals with the efforts of the Presbyterians to have their church system established by parliamentary authority as the national system after the abolition of the episcopate of the Church of England in 1643. 3 **Pluralitie** the holding of more than one post by the same minister 7 **classic Hierarchy** the authorities of a classis, synod or council, made up of the ministers and elders of a district 8 **A.S.** Adam Stuart **Rotherford** Samuel Rutherford, both Scots Presbyterian ministers influential in England, authors of pamphlets urging the adoption of the Scots system **Edwards** Thomas, an English Presbyterian pamphleteer 14 **Trent** the Council of Trent, called by the Pope in the sixteenth century after the Protestant reformations 17 **Phylacteries** parchments containing phrases from the Law worn by pious and legalistic Jews **bauk** spare 20 Priest is a contraction of presbyter

Comus

A MASK

THE PERSONS

The ATTENDANT SPIRIT   1. BROTHER
     afterwards in the habit of Thyrsis   2. BROTHER
COMUS with his crew   SABRINA THE NYMPH
THE LADY

The first Scene discovers a wilde Wood.
The ATTENDANT SPIRIT *descends or enters.*

Before the starry threshold of *Joves* Court
My mansion is, where those immortal shapes
Of bright aëreal Spirits live insphear'd
In Regions milde of calm and serene Ayr,
Above the smoak and stirr of this dim spot,
Which men call Earth, and with low-thoughted care
Confin'd, and pester'd in this pin-fold here,
Strive to keep up a frail, and Feaverish being
Unmindfull of the crown that Vertue gives
After this mortal change, to her true Servants   10
Amongst the enthron'd gods on Sainted seats.
Yet som there be that by due steps aspire
To lay their just hands on that Golden Key
That ope's the Palace of Eternity:
To such my errand is, and but for such,
I would not soil these pure Ambrosial weeds,
With the rank vapours of this Sin-worn mould.
    But to my task. *Neptune* besides the sway
Of every salt Flood, and each ebbing Stream,

A Mask, so entitled by Milton but since the early eighteenth century commonly entitled COMUS, was first presented at Ludlow Castle in 1634 before the Earl of Bridgewater as part of the celebrations at his taking up of the office of Lord President (or Governor) of Wales, his daughter and two sons playing the parts of the Lady and the Brothers, and his music-master, Henry Lawes, that of the Attendant Spirit. **3 insphear'd** see "Christ's Nativity," 125 and "Il Penseroso," 89-96 **7 pester'd** shackled **pin-fold** enclosure for stray animals **11 sainted seats** see Revelation IV: 4 **16 Ambrosial weeds** heavenly garments **17 mould** substance

20 Took in by lot 'twixt high, and neather *Jove,*
Imperial rule of all the Sea-girt Iles
That like to rich, and various gemms inlay
The unadorned boosom of the Deep,
Which he to grace his tributary gods
By course commits to severall goverment,
And gives them leave to wear their Saphire crowns,
And weild their little tridents, but this Ile
The greatest, and the best of all the main
He quarters to his blu-hair'd deities,
30 And all this tract that fronts the falling Sun
A noble Peer of mickle trust, and power
Has in his charge, with temper'd awe to guide
An old, and haughty Nation proud in Arms:
Where his fair off-spring nurs't in Princely lore,
Are coming to attend their Fathers state,
And new-entrusted Scepter, but their way
Lies through the perplex't paths of this drear Wood,
The nodding horror of whose shady brows
Threats the forlorn and wandring Passinger.
40 And here their tender age might suffer perill,
But that by quick command from Soveran *Jove*
I was dispatcht for their defence, and guard;
And listen why, for I will tell ye now
What never yet was heard in Tale or Song
From old, or modern Bard in Hall, or Bowr.
    Bacchus that first from out the purple Grape,
Crush't the sweet poyson of mis-used Wine
After the *Tuscan* Mariners transform'd
Coasting the *Tyrrhene* shore, as the winds listed,
50 On *Circes* Iland fell (who knows not *Circe*
The daughter of the Sun? Whose charmed Cup
Whoever tasted, lost his upright shape,
And downward fell into a groveling Swine)

20 **high and neather Jove** Zeus (Jupiter), god of the sky, and
Pluto, god of the underworld, brothers of Neptune, god of the
sea 29 **quarters to** divides among 30 **this tract** Wales and the
bordering English counties 31 **Peer** Earl of Bridgewater **mickle**
great 37 **perplex't** tangled 48 Bacchus was said to have trans-
formed into dolphins some mariners who kidnapped him. 50 The
story of Circe and her enchantment of the crew of Ulysses is told
by Homer, *Odyssey,* x.

This Nymph that gaz'd upon his clustring locks,
With Ivy berries wreath'd, and his blithe youth,
Had by him, ere he parted thence, a Son
Much like his Father, but his Mother more,
Whom therfore she brought up and *Comus* nam'd,
Who ripe, and frolick of his full grown age,
Roaving the *Celtick*, and *Iberian* fields,   60
At last betakes him to this ominous Wood,
And in thick shelter of black shades imbowr'd,
Excells his Mother at her mighty Art,
Offring to every weary Travailer,
His orient liquor in a Crystal Glasse,
To quench the drouth of *Phœbus*, which as they taste
(For most do taste through fond intemperate thirst)
Soon as the Potion works, their human count'nance,
Th' express resemblance of the gods, is chang'd
Into som brutish form of Woolf, or Bear,   70
Or Ounce, or Tiger, Hog, or bearded Goat,
All other parts remaining as they were,
And they, so perfect in their misery,
Not once perceive their foul disfigurement,
But boast themselves more comely then before
And all their friends, and native home forget
To roule with pleasure in a sensual stie.
Therfore when any favour'd of high *Jove,*
Chances to passe through this adventrous glade,
Swift as the Sparkle of a glancing Star,   80
I shoot from Heav'n to give him safe convoy,
As now I do: But first I must put off
These my skie robes spun out of *Iris* Wooff,
And take the Weeds and likenes of a Swain,
That to the service of this house belongs,
Who with his soft Pipe, and smooth-dittied Song,
Well knows to still the wilde winds when they roar,
And hush the waving Woods, nor of lesse faith,
And in this office of his Mountain watch,
Likeliest, and neerest to the present ayd   90
Of this occasion. But I hear the tread
Of hatefull steps, I must be viewles now.

60 Celtick French **Iberian** Spanish **65 orient** sparkling **66 Phoebus** sun **71 Ounce** a kind of lynx **83 Iris** rainbow goddess **92 viewless** invisible

Comus *enters with a Charming Rod in one hand, his Glass in the*
other, with him a rout of Monsters headed like sundry sorts
of wilde Beasts, but otherwise like Men and Women, their
Apparel glistring, they com in making a riotous and unruly
noise, with Torches in their hands.

Comus. The Star that bids the Shepherd fold,
Now the top of Heav'n doth hold,
And the gilded Car of Day,
His glowing Axle doth allay
In the steep *Atlantick* stream,
And the slope Sun his upward beam
Shoots against the dusky Pole,
100 Pacing toward the other gole
Of his Chamber in the East.
Mean while welcom Joy, and Feast,
Midnight shout, and revelry,
Tipsie dance, and Jollity.
Braid your Locks with rosie Twine
Dropping odours, dropping Wine.
Rigor now is gon to bed,
And Advice with scrupulous head,
Strict Age, and sowre Severity,
110 With their grave Saws in slumber ly.
We that are of purer fire
Imitate the Starry Quire,
Who in their nightly watchfull Sphears,
Lead in swift round the Months and Years.
The Sounds, and Seas with all their finny drove
Now to the Moon in wavering Morrice move,
And on the Tawny Sands and Shelves,
Trip the pert Fairies and the dapper Elves;
By dimpled Brook, and Fountain brim,
120 The Wood-Nymphs deckt with Daisies trim,
Their merry wakes and pastimes keep:
What hath night to do with sleep?
Night hath better sweets to prove,
Venus now wakes, and wak'ns Love.
Com let us our rights begin,
Tis onely day-light that makes Sin
Which these dun shades will ne'er report.

105 **rosy twine** twined roses   110 **saws** maxims   **116 Morrice**
grotesque dance   125 **rights** rites

Hail Goddesse of Nocturnal sport
Dark vaild *Cotytto*, t' whom the secret flame
Of mid-night Torches burns; mysterious Dame   130
That ne're art call'd, but when the Dragon woom
Of Stygian darknes spets her thickest gloom,
And makes one blot of all the ayr,
Stay thy cloudy Ebon chair,
Wherin thou rid'st with *Hecat'*, and befriend
Us thy vow'd Priests, till utmost end
Of all thy dues be done, and none left out,
Ere the blabbing Eastern scout,
The nice Morn on th' *Indian* steep
From her cabin'd loop hole peep,   146
And to the tel-tale Sun discry
Our conceal'd Solemnity.
Com, knit hands, and beat the ground,
In a light fantastick round.

The Measure.

Break off, break off, I feel the different pace,
Of som chast footing neer about this ground.
Run to your shrouds, within these Brakes and Trees,
Our number may affright: Som Virgin sure
(For so I can distinguish by mine Art)
Benighted in these Woods. Now to my charms,   150
And to my wily trains, I shall e're long
Be well stock't with as fair a herd as graz'd
About my Mother *Circe*. Thus I hurl
My dazling Spells into the spungy ayr,
Of power to cheat the eye with blear illusion,
And give it false presentments, lest the place
And my quaint habits breed astonishment,
And put the Damsel to suspicious flight,
Which must not be, for that's against my course;
I under fair pretence of friendly ends,   160
And well plac't words of glozing courtesie
Baited with reasons not unplausible

129 **Cotytto** a Thracian goddess of immodesty, worshipped **at** night in riotous festivals 132 **Stygian** of the Styx, river in Hades **spets** spits 135 **Hecat'** Hecate, goddess of sorcery, associated with the moon 139 **nice** fastidious 147 **shrouds** hiding places 151 **trains** lures 154 **spungy** absorbent 157 **habits** dress 161 **glozing** flattering

Wind me into the easie-hearted man,
And hugg him into snares. When once her eye
Hath met the vertue of this Magick dust,
I shall appear som harmles Villager
Whom thrift keeps up about his Country gear,
But here she comes, I fairly step aside
And hearken, if I may, her business here.

THE LADY *enters.*

170 This way the noise was, if mine ear be true,
My best guide now, me thought it was the sound
Of Riot, and ill manag'd Merriment,
Such as the jocond Flute, or gamesom Pipe
Stirs up among the loose unleter'd Hinds,
When for their teeming Flocks, and granges full
In wanton dance they praise the bountous *Pan,*
And thank the gods amiss. I should be loath
To meet the rudenesse, and swill'd insolence
Of such late Wassailers; yet O where els
180 Shall I inform my unacquainted feet
In the blind mazes of this tangl'd Wood?
My Brothers when they saw me wearied out
With this long way, resolving here to lodge
Under the spreading favour of these Pines,
Stept as they se'd to the next Thicket side
To bring me Berries, or such cooling fruit
As the kind hospitable Woods provide.
They left me then, when the gray-hooded Eev'n
Like a sad Votarist in Palmers weed
190 Rose from the hindmost wheels of *Phœbus* wain.
But where they are, and why they came not back,
Is now the labour of my thoughts, 'tis likeliest
They had ingag'd their wandring steps too far,
And envious darknes, e're they could return,
Had stole them from me, els O theevish Night
Why shouldst thou, but for som fellonious end,

165 **verute** power 167-69 *1645; 1673 reads*: "And hearken, if I may, her business here./ But here she comes, I fairly step aside"/ 167 **gear** business 174 **Hinds** farm laborers 176 **Pan** god of nature 178 **swill'd** drunken 179 **Wassailers** revellers 189 **sad** serious **Votarist** person who has taken a religious vow **Palmers weed** pilgrim s habit

In thy dark lantern thus close up the Stars,
That nature hung in Heav'n, and fill'd their Lamps
With everlasting oil, to give due light
To the misled and lonely Travailer?   200
This is the place, as well as I may guess,
Whence eev'n now the tumult of loud Mirth
Was rife, and perfet in my list'ning ear,
Yet nought but single darknes do I find.
What might this be? A thousand fantasies
Begin to throng into my memory
Of calling shapes, and beckning shadows dire,
And airy tongues, that syllable mens names
On Sands, and Shoars, and desert Wildernesses.
These thoughts may startle well, but not astound   210
The vertuous mind, that ever walks attended
By a strong siding champion Conscience.——
O welcom pure-ey'd Faith, white-handed Hope,
Thou hovering Angel girt with golden wings,
And thou unblemish't form of Chastity,
I see ye visibly, and now beleeve
That he, the Supreme good, t' whom all things ill
Are but as slavish officers of vengeance,
Would send a glistring Guardian if need were
To keep my life and honour unassail'd.   220
Was I deceiv'd, or did a sable cloud
Turn forth her silver lining on the night?
I did not err, there does a sable cloud
Turn forth her silver lining on the night,
And casts a gleam over this tufted Grove.
I cannot hallow to my Brothers, but
Such noise as I can make to be heard farthest
Ile venter. for my new enliv'nd spirits
Prompt me; and they perhaps are not far off.

SONG

Sweet Echo, sweetest Nymph that liv'st unseen   230
Within thy airy shell

203 **perfet** perfectly clear 204 **single** complete 230-43 The
nymph Echo pined away on the death of her lover Narcissus un-
til she was nothing but a voice haunting the air in such spots
as the river Meander in Phyrigia or the valleys of the nightin-
gales near Athens. She is daughter of the sphere because she

By slow Meander's *margent green,*
And in the violet-imbroider'd vale
Where the love-lorn Nightingale
Nightly to thee her sad Song mourneth well.
Canst thou not tell me of a gentle Pair
That likest thy Narcissus are?
O if thou have
Hid them in som flowry Cave,
240 *Tell me but where*
Sweet Queen of Parly, Daughter of the Sphear,
So maist thou be translated to the skies,
And give resounding grace to all Heav'ns Harmonies.

Com. Can any mortal mixture of Earths mould
Breath such Divine inchanting ravishment?
Sure somthing holy lodges in that brest,
And with these raptures moves the vocal air
To testifie his hidd'n residence;
How sweetly did they float upon the wings
250 Of silence, through the empty-vaulted night
At every fall smoothing the Raven doune
Of darknes till it smil'd: I have oft heard
My mother *Circe* with the Sirens three,
Amidst the flowry-kirtl'd *Naiades*
Culling their Potent hearbs, and balefull drugs,
Who as they sung, would take the prison'd soul,
And lap it in *Elysium, Scylla* wept,
And chid her barking waves into attention,
And fell *Charybdis* murmur'd soft applause:
260 Yet they in pleasing slumber lull'd the sense,
And in sweet madnes rob'd it of it self,
But such a sacred, and home-felt delight,
Such sober certainty of waking bliss
I never heard till now. Ile speak to her

dwells in the shell or vault of the heavens; and she was associated in Greek myth with the music of the spheres (see "Christ's Nativity," 125). 242 **translated** raised aloft 251 **fall** cadence 253 **Sirens** singing maidens who tempted seamen to their deaths, *Odyssey* XII 254 **kirtled** skirted **Naiades** water nymphs 257 **Elysium** Paradise **Scylla** a dangerous rock in the straits between Italy and Sicily, represented in classical legend as a female monster 258 **Charybdis** a whirlpool in the same straits

And she shall be my Queen. Hail forren wonder
Whom certain these rough shades did never breed
Unlesse the Goddes that in rurall shrine
Dwell'st here with *Pan*, or *Silvan*, by blest Song
Forbidding every bleak unkindly Fog
To touch the prosperous growth of this tall Wood.   270
   La. Nay gentle Shepherd ill is lost that praise
That is addrest to unattending Ears,
Not any boast of skill, but extreme shift
How to regain my sever'd company
Compell'd me to awake the courteous Echo
To give me answer from her mossie Couch.
     Co. What chance good Lady hath bereft you thus?
     La. Dim darknes, and this leavy Labyrinth.
     Co. Could that divide you from neer-ushering guides?
     La. They left me weary on a grassie terf.   280
     Co. By falshood, or discourtesie, or why?
     La. To seek i'th vally som cool friendly Spring.
     Co. And left your fair side all unguarded Lady?
     La. They were but twain, and purpos'd quick return.
     Co. Perhaps fore-stalling night prevented them.
     La. How easie my misfortune is to hit!
     Co. Imports their loss, beside the present need?
     La. No less then if I should my brothers loose.
     Co. Were they of manly prime, or youthful bloom?
     La. As smooth as *Hebe*'s their unrazor'd lips.   290
     Co. Two such I saw, what time the labour'd Oxe
In his loose traces from the furrow came,
And the swink't hedger at his Supper sate;
I saw them under a green mantling vine
That crawls along the side of yon small hill,
Plucking ripe clusters from the tender shoots,
Their port was more than human, as they stood;
I took it for a faëry vision
Of som gay creatures of the element
That in the colours of the Rainbow live   300
And play i'th plighted clouds. I was aw-strook,
And as I past, I worship; if those you seek
It were a journey like the path to Heav'n,
To help you find them. La. Gentle villager

268 **Pan, Silvan** nature gods 290 **Hebe** goddess of youth
293 **swink't** wearied with labor 297 **port** bearing 299 **element**
air or sky 301 **plighted** folded

What readiest way would bring me to that place?
   Co. Due west it rises from this shrubby point.
   LA. To find out that, good Shepherd, I suppose,
In such a scant allowance of Star-light,
Would overtask the best Land-Pilots art,
310 Without the sure guess of well-practiz'd feet.
   Co. I know each lane, and every alley green
Dingle, or bushy dell of this wilde Wood,
And every bosky bourn from side to side
My daily walks and ancient neighbourhood,
And if your stray attendance be yet lodg'd,
Or shroud within these limits, I shall know
Ere morrow wake, or the low-roosted lark
From her thatch't pallat rowse, if otherwise
I can conduct you Lady to a low
320 But loyal cottage, where you may be safe
Till further quest'. LA. Shepherd I take thy word,
And trust thy honest offer'd courtesie,
Which oft is sooner found in lowly sheds
With smoaky rafters, then in tapstry Halls
And Courts of Princes, where it first was nam'd,
And yet is most pretended: In a place
Less warranted then this, or less secure
I cannot be, that I should fear to change it.
Eie me blest Providence, and square my triall
330 To my proportiond'd strength. Shepherd lead on.——

THE TWO BROTHERS.

   ELD. BRO. Unmuffle ye faint stars, and thou fair Moon
That wontst to love the travailers benizon,
Stoop thy pale visage through an amber cloud,
And disinherit *Chaos,* that raigns here
In double night of darknes, and of shades;
Or if your influence be quite damm'd up
With black usurping mists, som gentle taper
Though a rush Candle from the wicker hole
Of som clay habitation visit us
340 With thy long levell'd rule of streaming light,

312 **dingle** hollow 313 **bosky bourn** shrub-bordered stream
316 **shroud** shelter 327 **warranted** protected 329 **square** adjust
331 **wontst** art accustomed **benizon** blessing

And thou shalt be our star of *Arcady*,
Or *Tyrian* Cynosure. 2. BRO. Or if our eyes
Be barr'd that happines, might we but hear
The folded flocks pen'd in their watled cotes,
Or sound of pastoral reed with oaten stops,
Or whistle from the Lodge, or village cock
Count the night watches to his feathery Dames,
'Twould be som solace yet, som little chearing
In this close dungeon of innumerous bowes.
But O that haples virgin our lost sister   350
Where may she wander now, whether betake her
From the chill dew, amongst rude burrs and thistles?
Perhaps som cold bank is her boulster now
Or 'gainst the rugged bark of som broad Elm
Leans her unpillow'd head fraught with sad fears.
What if in wild amazement, and affright,
Or while we speak within the direfull grasp
Of Savage hunger, or of Savage heat?
    ELD. BRO. Peace brother, be not over-exquisite
To cast the fashion of uncertain evils;   360
For grant they be so, while they rest unknown,
What need a man forestall his date of grief,
And run to meet what he would most avoid?
Or if they be but false alarms of Fear,
How bitter is such self-delusion?
I do not think my sister so to seek,
Or so unprincipl'd in vertues book,
And the sweet peace that goodnes boosoms ever,
As that the single want of light and noise
(Not being in danger, as I trust she is not)   370
Could stir the constant mood of her calm thoughts,
And put them into mis-becoming plight.
Vertue could see to do what vertue would
By her own radiant light, though Sun and Moon
Were in the flat Sea sunk. And Wisdoms self
Oft seeks to sweet retired Solitude,

341 **star of Arcady** Calisto, an Arcadian nymph, turned into the
constellation Great Bear by Jupiter 342 **Tyrian Cynosure** pole-
star, by which the Phoenicians navigated 343 **watled cotes**
sheepfolds made of stakes and twigs 345 **pastoral . . . stops**
traditional shepherd's pipe 349 **innumerous** innumerable
359 **over-exquisite** over-subtle 360 **cast the fashion** forecast the
nature 366 **to seek** at a loss 369 **single** mere 376 **seeks resorts**

Where with her best nurse Contemplation
She plumes her feathers, and lets grow her wings
That in the various bussle of resort
380 Were all to ruffl'd, and somtimes impair'd.
He that has light within his own cleer brest
May sit i'th center, and enjoy bright day,
But he that hides a dark soul, and foul thoughts
Benighted walks under the mid-day Sun;
Himself is his own dungeon.
        2. Bro. Tis most true
That musing meditation most affects
The Pensive secrecy of desert cell,
Far from the cheerfull haunt of men, and herds,
390 And sits as safe as in a Senat house,
For who would rob a Hermit of his Weeds,
His few Books, or his Beads, or Maple Dish,
Or do his gray hairs any violence?
But beauty like the fair Hesperian Tree
Laden with blooming gold, had need the guard
Of dragon watch with uninchanted eye,
To save her blossoms, and defend her fruit
From the rash hand of bold Incontinence.
You may as well spred out the unsun'd heaps
400 Of Misers treasure by an out-laws den,
And tell me it is safe, as bid me hope
Danger will wink on Opportunity,
And let a single helpless maiden pass
Uninjur'd in this wilde surrounding wast.
Of night, or lonelines it recks me not,
I fear the dred events that dog them both,
Lest som ill greeting touch attempt the person
Of our unowned sister.
        Eld. Bro. I do not, brother,
410 Inferr, as if I thought my sisters state
Secure without all doubt, or controversie:
Yet where an equall poise of hope and fear

379 **resort** crowded places 382 **centre** of the earth 392 *Beads*
rosary 394 The **Hesperian Tree** tree bearing golden apples in
the mythical gardens of Hesperus, ruler of the west and evening
star, was guarded by his three daughters, the Hesperides, and by
a dragon conquered by Hercules. 405 **recks** concerns 408 **un-
owned** unaccompanied

Does arbitrate th'event, my nature is
That I encline to hope, rather then fear,
And gladly banish squint suspicion.
My sister is not so defenceless left
As you imagine, she has a hidden strength
Which you remember not.
    2. Bro. What hidden strength,
Unless the strength of Heav'n, if you mean that?   420
    Eld. Bro. I mean that too, but yet a hidden strength
Which if Heav'n gave it, may be term'd her own:
'Tis chastity, my brother, chastity:
She that has that, is clad in compleat steel,
And like a quiver'd Nymph with Arrows keen
May trace huge Forests, and unharbour'd Heaths,
Infamous Hills, and sandy perilous wildes,
Where through the sacred rayes of Chastity,
No savage fierce, Bandite, or mountaneer
Will dare to soyl her Virgin purity,   430
Yea there, where very desolation dwels
By grots, and caverns shag'd with horrid shades,
She may pass on with unblench't majesty,
Be it not don in pride, or in presumption.
Som say no evil thing that walks by night
In fog, or fire, by lake, or moorish fen,
Blew meager Hag, or stubborn unlaid ghost,
That breaks his magick chains at *curfeu* time,
No goblin, or swart Faëry of the mine,
Hath hurtfull power o're true virginity.   440
Do ye beleeve me yet, or shall I call
Antiquity from the old Schools of Greece
To testifie the arms of Chastity?
Hence had the huntress *Dian* her dred bow
Fair silver-shafted Queen for ever chaste,
Wherwith she tam'd the brinded lioness
And spotted mountain pard, but set at nought
The frivolous bolt of *Cupid,* gods and men
Fear'd her stern frown, and she was queen oth' Woods.
What was that snaky-headed *Gorgon* sheild   450

413 **arbitrate the event** determine the outcome 425 **Nymph**
nymph of Diana, goddess of chastity 426 **unharbour'd** shelter-
less 431 **very** absolute 433 **unblenched** unfaltering 439 **swart**
swarthy 446 **brinded** tawny with streaks 447 **pard** leopard
448 **bolt** arrow

That wise *Minerva* wore, unconquer'd Virgin,
Wherwith she freez'd her foes to congeal'd stone?
But rigid looks of Chast austerity,
And noble grace that dash't brute violence
With sudden adoration, and blank aw.
So dear to Heav'n is Saintly chastity,
That when a soul is found sincerely so,
A thousand liveried Angels lacky her,
Driving far off each thing of sin and guilt,
460 And in cleer dream, and solemn vision
Tell her of things that no gross ear can hear,
Till oft convers with heav'nly habitants
Begin to cast a beam on th'outward shape,
The unpolluted temple of the mind,
And turns it by degrees to the souls essence,
Till all be made immortal: but when lust
By unchaste looks, loose gestures, and foul talk,
But most by leud and lavish act of sin,
Lets in defilement to the inward parts,
470 The soul grows clotted by contagion,
Imbodies, and imbrutes, till she quite loose
The divine property of her first being.
Such are those thick and gloomy shadows damp
Oft seen in Charnell vaults, and Sepulchers
Lingering, and sitting by a new made grave,
As loath to leave the body that it lov'd,
And link't it self by carnal sensualty
To a degenerate and degraded state.
    2. Bro. How charming is divine Philosophy!
480 Not harsh, and crabbed as dull fools suppose,
But musical as is *Apollo*'s lute,
And a perpetual feast of nectar'd sweets,
Where no crude surfet raigns. Eld. Bro. List, list, I hear
Som far off hallow break the silent Air.
    2. Bro. Me thought so too; what should it be?

451-3 **Minerva,** goddess of wisdom, carried a shield bearing the head of Medusa, one of the Gorgon sisters who had snakes for hair and whose look petrified the beholder. 458 **liveried** wearing livery, distinctive clothing of an attendant **lacky** attend 472 **property** quality 456-478 The passage is full of echoes of Plato's discussion of the soul in the dialogue *Phaedo* (especially 80-1) and of such scriptural passages as John ii: 21, I corinthians iii: 17, Psalms li: 6.

ELD. BRO. For certain
Either som one like us night-founder'd here,
Or els som neighbour Wood-man, or at worst,
Som roaving Robber calling to his fellows.

    2. BRO. Heav'n keep my sister, agen agen and neer,   490
Best draw, and stand upon our guard.

    ELD. BRO. Ile hallow,
If he be friendly he comes well, if not,
Defence is a good cause, and Heav'n be for us.

The ATTENDANT SPIRIT *habited like a Shepherd.*

That hallow I should know, what are you? speak;
Com not too neer, you fall on iron stakes else.

    SPIR. What voice is that, my young Lord? speak agen.

    2. BRO. O brother, 'tis my father Shepherd sure.

    ELD. BRO. *Thyrsis?* Whose artful strains have oft delaid
The huddling brook to hear his madrigal,   500
And sweeten'd every muskrose of the dale,
How cam'st thou here good Swain? hath any ram
Slip't from the fold, or young Kid lost his dam,
Or straggling weather the pen't flock forsook?
How couldst thou find this dark sequester'd nook?

    SPIR. O my lov'd masters heir, and his next joy,
I came not here on such a trivial toy
As a stray'd Ewe, or to pursue the stealth
Of pilfering Woolf, not all the fleecy wealth
That doth enrich these Downs, is worth a thought   510
To this my errand, and the care it brought.
But O my Virgin Lady, where is she?
How chance she is not in your company?

    ELD. BRO. To tell thee sadly Shepherd, without blame,
Or our neglect, we lost her as we came.

    SPIR. Ay me unhappy then my fears are true.

    ELD. BRO. What fears good *Thyrsis?* Prethee briefly shew.

    SPIR. Ile tell ye, 'tis not vain, or fabulous,
(Though so esteem'd by shallow ignorance)
What the sage Poëts taught by th' heav'nly Muse,   520
Storied of old in high immortal vers
Of dire *Chimera's* and inchanted Iles,
And rifted Rocks whose entrance leads to hell,

498 **father** father's 506 **next** dearest 507 **toy** trifle 522 **Chimera** legendary fire-breathing monster

For such there be, but unbelief is blind.
   Within the navil of this hideous Wood,
Immur'd in cypress shades a Sorcerer dwels
Of *Bacchus,* and of *Circe* born, great *Comus,*
Deep skill'd in all his mothers witcheries,
And here to every thirsty wanderer,
530 By sly enticement gives his banefull cup,
With many murmurs mixt, whose pleasing poison
The visage quite transforms of him that drinks,
And the inglorious likenes of a beast
Fixes instead, unmoulding reasons mintage
Character'd in the face; this have I learn't
Tending my flocks hard by i'th hilly crofts,
That brow this bottom glade, whence night by night
He and his monstrous rout are heard to howl
Like stabl'd wolves, or tigers at their prey,
540 Doing abhorred rites to *Hecate*
In their obscured haunts of inmost bowres.
Yet have they many baits, and guilefull spells
To inveigle and invite th'unwary sense
Of them that pass unweeting by the way.
This evening late by then the chewing flocks
Had ta'n their supper on the savoury Herb
Of Knot-grass dew-besprent, and were in fold,
I sate me down to watch upon a bank
With Ivy canopied, and interwove
550 With flaunting Hony-suckle, and began
Wrapt in a pleasing fit of melancholy
To meditate my rural minstrelsie,
Till fancy had her fill, but ere a close
The wonted roar was up amidst the Woods,
And fill'd the Air with barbarous dissonance,
At which I ceas't, and listen'd them a while,
Till an unusuall stop of sudden silence
Gave respit to the drowsie frighted steeds
That draw the litter of close-curtain'd sleep.
560 At last a soft and solemn breathing sound
Rose like a steam of rich distill'd Perfumes,
And stole upon the Air, that even Silence

525 **navil** centre 531 **murmurs** incantations 534 **mintage stamp**
535 **Character'd** engraved 536 **crofts** fields 537 **brow** overlook
544 **unweeting** unknowingly 552 **meditate** practise 553 **ere a
close** before the end of a phrase 554 **wonted** usual

Was took e're she was ware, and wish't she might
Deny her nature, and be never more
Still to be so displac't. I was all eare,
And took in strains that might create a soul
Under the ribs of Death, but O ere long
Too well I did perceive it was the voice
Of my most honour'd Lady, your dear sister.
Amaz'd I stood, harrow'd with grief and fear,   570
And O poor hapless Nightingale thought I,
How sweet thou sing'st, how neer the deadly snare!
Then down the Lawns I ran with headlong hast
Through paths, and turnings oft'n trod by day,
Till guided by mine ear I found the place
Where that damn'd wisard hid in sly disguise
(For so by certain signes I knew) had met
Already, ere my best speed could prævent,
The aidless innocent Lady his wish't prey,
Who gently ask't if he had seen such two,   580
Supposing him som neighbour villager;
Longer I durst not stay, but soon I guess't
Ye were the two she mean't, with that I sprung
Into swift flight, till I had found you here,
But furder know I not. 2. BRO. O night and shades,
How are ye joyn'd with hell in triple knot
Against th'unarmed weakness of one Virgin
Alone, and helpless! Is this the confidence
You gave me Brother? ELD. BRO. Yes, and keep it still,
Lean on it safely, not a period   590
Shall be unsaid for me: against the threats
Of malice or of sorcery, or that power
Which erring men call Chance, this I hold firm,
Vertue may be assail'd, but never hurt,
Surpriz'd by unjust force, but not enthrall'd,
Yea even that which mischief meant most harm,
Shall in the happy trial prove most glory.
But evil on it self shall back recoyl,
And mix no more with goodness, when at last
Gather'd like scum, and setl'd to it self   600
It shall be in eternal restless change
Self-fed, and self-consum'd, if this fail,
The pillar'd firmament is rott'nness,

563 **took** charmed   590 **period** sentence   591 **for me** for my part

And earths base built on stubble. But com let's on.
Against th' opposing will and arm of Heav'n
May never this just sword be lifted up,
But for that damn'd magician, let him be girt
With all the greisly legions that troop
Under the sooty flag of *Acheron,*
610 *Harpyies* and *Hydra's,* or all the monstrous forms
'Twixt *Africa* and *Inde,* Ile find him out,
And force him to restore his purchase back,
Or drag him by the curls, to a foul death,
Curs'd as his life.

    SPIR. Alas good ventrous youth,
I love thy courage yet, and bold Emprise,
But here thy sword can do thee little stead,
Farr other arms, and other weapons must
Be those that quell the might of hellish charms,
620 He with his bare wand can unthred thy joynts,
And crumble all thy sinews.

    ELD. BRO. Why prethee Shepherd
How durst thou then thy self approach so neer
As to make this relation?

    SPIR. Care and utmost shifts
How to secure the Lady from surprisal,
Brought to my mind a certain Shepherd Lad
Of small regard to see to, yet well skill'd
In every vertuous plant and healing herb
630 That spreds her verdant leaf to th'morning ray,
He lov'd me well, and oft would beg me sing,
Which when I did, he on the tender grass
Would sit, and hearken even to extasie,
And in requitall ope his leather'n scrip,
And shew me simples of a thousand names
Telling their strange and vigorous faculties;
Amongst the rest a small unsightly root,
But of divine effect, he cull'd me out;
The leaf was darkish, and had prickles on it,
640 But in another Countrey, as he said,
Bore a bright golden flowre, but not in this soyl:
Unknown, and like esteem'd, and the dull swayn

609 **Acheron** river of Hades 612 **purchase** booty 617 **stead**
service 628 **see to** behold 629 **vertuous** potent for good
634 **scrip** pouch 635 **simples** medicinal herbs 636 **faculties**
powers 642 **like esteem'd** correspondingly valued

Treads on it daily with his clouted shoon,
And yet more med'cinal is it then that *Moly*
That *Hermes* once to wise *Ulysses* gave;
He call'd it *Hæmony,* and gave it me,
And bad me keep it as of sovran use
'Gainst all inchantments, mildew blast, or damp
Or gastly furies apparition;
I purs't it up, but little reck'ning made,   650
Till now that this extremity compell'd,
But now I find it true; for by this means
I knew the foul inchanter though disguis'd,
Enter'd the very lime-twigs of his spells,
And yet came off: if you have this about you
(As I will give you when we go) you may
Boldly assault the necromancers hall;
Where if he be, with dauntless hardihood,
And brandish't blade rush on him, break his glass
And shed the lushious liquor on the ground,   660
But sease his wand, though he and his curst crew
Feirce signe of battail make, and menace high,
Or like the sons of *Vulcan* vomit smoak,
Yet will they soon retire, if he but shrink.
  ELD. BRO. *Thyrsis* lead on apace, Ile follow thee,
And som good angel bear a sheild before us.

*The Scene changes to a stately Palace, set out with all manner of
    deliciousness: soft Musick, Tables spred with all dainties.
    COMUS appears with his rabble, and the Lady set in an in-
    chanted Chair, to whom he offers his Glass, which she puts
    by, and goes about to rise.*

  COMUS. Nay Lady sit; if I but wave this wand,
Your nervs are all chain'd up in Alablaster,
And you a statue; or as *Daphne* was

643 **clouted** hobnailed or mended 644 **Moly,** the herb given
Ulysses by the god Hermes to protect him against Circe's temp-
tations (*Odyssey,* X, 302-6), was a symbol of temperance, Milton's
herb being even more medicinal because it represents chastity
646 **Haemony,** a name invented by Milton, from Haemonia,
ancient Thrace, alludes to a story in Plato's *Charmides,* 157, of
a Thracian physician whose unusual skill came from his knowl-
edge of the relation between bodily health and the health and
virtue of the soul. 654 **lime-twigs** twigs smeared with sticky
stuff to catch birds 663 **Vulcan** god of fire 669 **Daphne** nymph
who was changed into a laurel tree when pursued by Apollo

670 Root-bound, that fled *Apollo*.
    LA. Fool do not boast,
Thou canst not touch the freedom of my minde
With all thy charms, although this corporal rinde
Thou haste immanacl'd, while Heav'n sees good.
    Co. Why are you vext Lady? why do you frown?
Here dwel no frowns, nor anger, from these gates
Sorrow flies farr: See here be all the pleasures
That fancy can beget on youthfull thoughts,
When the fresh blood grows lively, and returns
680 Brisk as the *April* buds in Primrose-season.
And first behold this cordial Julep here
That flames, and dances in his crystal bounds
With spirits of balm, and fragrant Syrops mixt.
Not that *Nepenthes* which the wife of *Thone*,
In *Egypt* gave to *Jove*-born *Helena*
Is of such power to stir up joy as this,
To life so friendly, or so cool to thirst.
Why should you be so cruel to your self,
And to those dainty limms which nature lent
690 For gentle usage, and soft delicacy?
But you invert the cov'nants of her trust,
And harshly deal like an ill borrower
With that which you receiv'd on other terms,
Scorning the unexempt condition
By which all mortal frailty must subsist,
Refreshment after toil, ease after pain,
That have been tir'd all day without repast,
And timely rest have wanted, but fair Virgin
This will restore all soon.
700   LA. 'Twill not false traitor,
'Twill not restore the truth and honesty
That thou hast banish't from thy tongue with lies,
Was this the cottage, and the safe abode
Thou told'st me of? What grim aspects are these,
These oughly-headed Monsters? Mercy guard me!
Hence with thy brew'd inchantments, foul deceiver,
Hast thou betrai'd my credulous innocence
With visor'd falshood, and base forgery,

684 **Nepenthes** drink that banished sorrow, given Helen, daughter of Jove, by the wife of the Egyptian Thone after Troy war, *Odyssey*, IV 219-29 694 **unexempt** exempting no one 708 **visor'd** masked

And wouldst thou seek again to trap me here
With lickerish baits fit to ensnare a brute? 710
Were it a draft for *Juno* when she banquets,
I would not taste thy treasonous offer; none
But such as are good men can give good things,
And that which is not good, is not delicious
To a wel-govern'd and wise appetite.

    Co. O foolishnes of men! that lend their ears
To those budge doctors of the *Stoick* Furr,
And fetch their precepts from the *Cynick* Tub,
Praising the lean and sallow Abstinence.
Wherefore did Nature powre her bounties forth, 720
With such a full and unwithdrawing hand,
Covering the earth with odours, fruits, and flocks,
Thronging the Seas with spawn innumerable,
But all to please, and sate the curious taste?
And set to work millions of spinning Worms,
That in their green shops weave the smooth-hair'd silk
To deck her Sons, and that no corner might
Be vacant of her plenty, in her own loyns
She hutch't th'all-worship ore, and precious gems
To store her children with; if all the world 730
Should in a pet of temperance feed on Pulse,
Drink the clear stream, and nothing wear but Freize,
Th'all-giver would be unthank't, would be unprais'd,
Not half his riches known, and yet despis'd,
And we should serve him as a grudging master,
As a penurious niggard of his wealth,
And live like Natures bastards, not her sons,
Who would be quite surcharg'd with her own weight,
And strangl'd with her waste fertility;
Th'earth cumber'd, and the wing'd air dark't with plumes, 740
The herds would over-multitude their Lords,
The Sea o'refraught would swell, & th'unsought diamonds
Would so emblaze the forhead of the Deep,

717 **budge** kind of fur used on academic hoods **Stoick** of Stoicism, an Athenian and Roman philosophy inculcating the control of passion and appetite 718 **Cynick Tub** the tub in which Diogenes, Greek Cynic philosopher, lived to show his contempt of the world 729 **hutch't** enclosed 731 **pulse** soup made of peas, beans 732 **Freize** coarse woollen cloth 743 **Deep** depths of the earth

And so bestudd with Stars, that they below
Would grow inur'd to light, and com at last
To gaze upon the Sun with shameless brows.
List Lady be not coy, and be not cosen'd
With that same vaunted name Virginity,
Beauty is natures coyn, must not be hoorded,
750 But must be currant, and the good thereof
Consists in mutual and partak'n bliss,
Unsavoury in th'injoyment of it self
If you let slip time, like a neglected rose
It withers on the stalk with languish't head.
Beauty is natures brag, and must be shown
In courts, at feasts, and high solemnities
Where most may wonder at the workmanship;
It is for homely features to keep home,
They had their name thence; course complexions
760 And cheeks of sorry grain will serve to ply
The sampler, and to teize the huswifes wooll.
What need a vermeil-tinctur'd lip for that
Love-darting eyes, or tresses like the Morn?
There was another meaning in these gifts,
Think what, and be adviz'd, you are but young yet.
    LA. I had not thought to have unlockt my lips
In this unhallow'd air, but that this Jugler
Would think to charm my judgement, as mine eyes
Obtruding false rules pranckt in reasons garb.
770 I hate when vice can bolt her arguments,
And vertue has no tongue to check her pride:
Impostor do not charge most innocent nature,
As if she would her children should be riotous
With her abundance, she good cateress
Means her provision onely to the good
That live according to her sober laws,
And holy dictate of spare Temperance:
If every just man that now pines with want
Had but a moderate and beseeming share
780 Of that which lewdly-pamper'd Luxury
Now heaps upon som few with vast excess,
Natures full blessings would be well dispenc't
In unsuperfluous eeven proportion,

747 **coy** disdainful **cosen'd** deluded 760 **grain** hue 761 **teize** comb 769 **pranckt** decked 770 **bolt** refine

And she no whit encomber'd with her store,
And then the giver would be better thank't,
His praise due paid, for swinish gluttony
Ne're looks to Heav'n amidst his gorgeous feast,
But with besotted base ingratitude
Cramms, and blasphemes his feeder. Shall I go on?
Or have I said anough? To him that dares   790
Arm his profane tongue with contemptuous words
Against the Sun-clad power of Chastity,
Fain would I somthing say, yet to what end?
Thou hast nor Eare, nor Soul to apprehend
The sublime notion, and high mystery
That must be utter'd to unfold the sage
And serious doctrine of Virginity,
And thou art worthy that thou shouldst not know
More happines then this thy present lot.
Enjoy your deer Wit, and gay Rhetorick   800
That hath so well been taught her dazling fence,
Thou art not fit to hear thy self convinc't;
Yet should I try, the uncontrouled worth
Of this pure cause would kindle my rap't spirits
To such a flame of sacred vehemence,
That dumb things would be mov'd to sympathize,
And the brute Earth would lend her nerves, and shake,
Till all thy magick structures rear'd so high,
Were shatter'd into heaps o're thy false head.
    Co. She fables not, I feel that I do fear   810
Her words set off by som superior power;
And though not mortal, yet a cold shuddring dew
Dips me all o're, as when the wrath of *Jove*
Speaks thunder, and the chains of *Erebus*
To som of *Saturns* crew. I must dissemble,
And try her yet more strongly. Com, no more,
This is meer moral babble, and direct
Against the canon laws of our foundation;
I must not suffer this, yet 'tis but the lees
And setlings of a melancholy blood;   820
But this will cure all streight, one sip of this
Will bathe the drooping spirits in delight
Beyond the bliss of dreams. Be wise, and taste.—

792 Revelation xii: 1 814 **Erebus** Hades 815 **Saturns crew**
Titans who rebelled against Jove, supplanter of Saturn

The BROTHERS *rush in with Swords drawn, wrest his Glass out of
his hand, and break it against the ground; his rout make
signe of resistance, but are all driven in; The attendant
Spirit comes in.*

SPIR. What, have you let the false enchanter scape?
O ye mistook, ye should have snatcht his wand
And bound him fast; without his rod revers't,
And backward mutters of dissevering power,
We cannot free the Lady that sits here
In stony fetters fixt, and motionless;
830 Yet stay, be not disturb'd, now I bethink me,
Som other means I have which may be us'd,
Which once of *Meliboeus* old I learnt
The soothest Shepherd that ere pip't on plains.
    There is a gentle Nymph not farr from hence,
That with moist curb sways the smooth Severn stream,
Sabrina is her name, a Virgin pure,
Whilom she was the daughter of *Locrine,*
That had the Scepter from his father *Brute.*
She guiltless damsell flying the mad pursuit
840 Of her enraged stepdam *Guendolen,*
Commended her fair innocence to the flood
That stay'd her flight with his cross-flowing course.
The water Nymphs that in the bottom plaid,
Held up their pearled wrists and took her in,
Bearing her straight to aged *Nereus* Hall,
Who piteous of her woes, rear'd her lank head,
And gave her to his daughters to imbathe
In nectar'd lavers strew'd with Asphodil,

827 **backward mutterings** reversed incantations 832 **Meliboeus,**
a conventional pastoral name for a shepherd, here probably in-
dicates Edmund Spenser who had told (*The Faerie Queene,* **II,**
x, 14-19) the story of Sabrina Milton is about to use and who
referred to Chaucer as Tityrus, another such name. 833 **soothest**
truest 835 **sways** rules 836-52 An ancient British legend tells
how Locrine, son of the Trojan Brutus who colonized Britain,
deserted his wife Guendolin for Estrildis, by whom he had had a
daughter, Sabrina. Guendolin defeated Locrine in battle and
pursued Sabrina, who was drowned in the river Severn which
flows through Wales and was named after her. 837 **Whilom**
once 845 **Nereus** old man of the sea, father of water nymphs
848 **nectar'd lavers** baths of nectar **Asphodil** flower of immortality

And through the porch and inlet of each sense
Dropt in Ambrosial Oils till she reviv'd, 850
And underwent a quick immortal change
Made Goddess of the River; still she retains
Her maid'n gentlenes, and oft at Eeve
Visits the herds along the twilight meadows,
Helping all urchin blasts, and ill luck signes
That the shrewd medling Elfe delights to make,
Which she with pretious viold liquors heals.
For which the Shepherds at their festivals
Carrol her goodnes lowd in rustick layes,
And throw sweet garland wreaths into her stream 860
Of pancies, pinks, and gaudy Daffadils.
And, as the old Swain said, she can unlock
The clasping charm, and thaw the numming spell,
If she be right invok't in warbled Song,
For maid'nhood she loves, and will be swift
To aid a Virgin, such as was her self
In hard besetting need, this will I try
And adde the power of som adjuring verse.

SONG

Sabrina fair
Listen where thou art sitting 870
Under the glassie, cool, translucent wave,
In twisted braids of Lillies knitting
The loose train of thy amber-dropping hair,
Listen for dear honours sake,
Goddess of the silver lake,
Listen and save.

Listen and appear to us
In name of great *Oceanus,*
By the earth-shaking *Neptune's* mace,
And *Tethys* grave majestick pace, 880
By hoary *Nereus* wrincled look,

850 **Ambrosial** from ambrosia, the fragrant food of gods, which conferred immortality 855 **helping** curing **urchin blasts** blights produced by sprites in the form of hedgehogs 856 **shrewd** malicious 873 **amber** yellow 878 **Oceanus** god of the river supposed by the ancients to encircle the world 880 **Tethys** wife of Oceanus

And the *Carpathian* wisards hook,
By scaly *Tritons* winding shell,
And old sooth-saying *Glaucus* spell,
By *Leucothea's* lovely hands,
And her son that rules the strands,
By *Thetis* tinsel-slipper'd feet,
And the Songs of *Sirens* sweet,
By dead *Parthenope's* dear tomb,
890 And fair *Ligea's* golden comb,
Wherwith she sits on diamond rocks
Sleeking her soft alluring locks,
By all the *Nymphs* that nightly dance
Upon thy streams with wily glance,
Rise, rise, and heave thy rosie head
From thy coral-pav'n bed,
And bridle in thy headlong wave,
Till thou our summons answer'd have.

                   Listen and save.

     Sᴀʙʀɪɴᴀ *rises, attended by water-Nymphes, and sings.*

900   *By the rushy-fringed bank,*
Where grows the Willow and the Osier dank,
    My sliding Chariot stayes,
Thick set with Agat, and the azurn sheen
Of Turkis blew, and Emrauld green
    That in the channell strayes,
Whilst from off the waters fleet
Thus I set my printless feet
O're the Cowslips Velvet head,
    That bends not as I tread,
910 *Gentle swain at thy request*
    I am here.

882 **Carpathian wisards hook** sheephook of Proteus, prophet and shepherd of the sea-flocks, whose home was the island of Carpathos 883 **Tritons winding shell** curled or sounding horn of Neptune's merman herald 884 **sooth-saying** prophesying **Glaucus** another sea god and prophet 885 **Leucothea** plunged into the sea with one of her sons in flight from her mad husband, both becoming sea deities, she being associated with dawn 887 **Thetis** one of the sea nymphs 888 **Sirens** see above 253 889-90 **Parthenope, Ligea** sirens 904 **Turkis** turquoise 907 **printless** leaving no print

SPIR. Goddess dear
We implore thy powerful hand
To undoe the charmed band
Of true Virgin here distrest,
Through the force, and through the wile
Of unblest inchanter vile.
    SAB. Shepherd 'tis my office best
To help insnared chastity;
Brightest Lady look on me,   920
Thus I sprinkle on thy brest
Drops that from my fountain pure,
I have kept of pretious cure,
Thrice upon thy fingers tip,
Thrice upon thy rubied lip,
Next this marble venom'd seat
Smear'd with gumms of glutenous heat
I touch with chaste palms moist and cold,
Now the spell hath lost his hold;
And I must haste ere morning hour   930
To wait in *Amphitrite*'s bowr.

      SABRINA *descends, and* THE LADY *rises out of her seat.*

    SPIR. Virgin, daughter of *Locrine*
Sprung of old *Anchises* line,
May thy brimmed waves for this
Their full tribute never miss
From a thousand petty rills,
That tumble down the snowy hills:
Summer drouth, or singed air
Never scorch thy tresses fair,
Nor wet *Octobers* torrent flood   940
Thy molten crystal fill with mudd,
May thy billows rowl ashoar
The beryl, and the golden ore,
May thy lofty head be crown'd
With many a tower and terrass round,
And here and there thy banks upon
With Groves of myrrhe, and cinnamon.

931 **Amphitrite** goddess of sea, wife of Neptune 933 **Anchises**
Trojan, father of Aeneas, founder of Rome, and ancestor of
Brutus, founder of Britain

Com Lady while Heaven lends us grace,
Let us fly this cursed place,
950 Lest the Sorcerer us intice
With som other new device.
Not a waste, or needless sound
Till we com to holier ground,
I shall be your faithfull guide
Through this gloomy covert wide,
And not many furlongs thence
Is your Fathers residence,
Where this night are met in state
Many a friend to gratulate
960 His wish't presence, and beside
All the Swains that there abide,
With Jiggs, and rural dance resort,
We shall catch them at their sport,
And our sudden coming there
Will double all their mirth and chere;
Com let us haste, the Stars grow high,
But night sits monarch yct in the mid sky.

The Scene changes, presenting Ludlow *Town and the Presidents
Castle, then com in Countrey-Dancers, after them the at-
tendant Spirit, with the* Two Brothers *and* The Lady.

SONG

Spir. *Back Shepherds, back, anough your play,*
Till next Sun-shine holiday,
970 *Here be without duck or nod*
Other trippings to be trod
Of lighter toes, and such Court guise
As Mercury *did first devise*
With the mincing Dryades
On the Lawns, and on the Leas.

This second Song presents them to their father and mother.

Noble Lord, and Lady bright,
I have brought ye new delight,
Here behold so goodly grown

973-4 **Mercury** messenger of the gods and leader of the dancing
wood-nymphs or Driades 974 **mincing** daintily stepping

Three fair branches of your own, 980
Heav'n hath timely tri'd their youth,
Their faith, their patience, and their truth.
And sent them here through hard assays
With a crown of deathless Praise,
  To triumph in victorious dance
O're sensual Folly, and Intemperance.

The dances ended, THE SPIRIT *Epiloguizes.*

SPIR. To the Ocean now I fly,
And those happy climes that ly
Where day never shuts his eye,
Up in the broad fields of the sky:
There I suck the liquid ayr 990
All amidst the Gardens fair
Of *Hesperus,* and his daughters three
That sing about the golden tree:
Along the crisped shades and bowres
Revels the spruce and jocond Spring,
The Graces, and the rosie-boosom'd Howres,
Thither all their bounties bring,
That there eternal Summer dwels,
And West winds, with musky wing
About the cedar'n alleys fling 1000
Nard, and *Cassia's* balmy smels.
Iris there with humid bow,
Waters the odorous banks that blow
Flowers of more mingled hew
Then her purfl'd scarf can shew,
And drenches with *Elysian* dew
(List mortals, if your ears be true)
Beds of *Hyacinth,* and roses

982 **assays** trials 992 **Hesperus** see above 394 994 **crisped** curled by the breeze 996 **Graces** three nymphs attendant on Venus, goddess of love, representing beauty, brightness, joy 1001 **Nard** aromatic balsam **Cassia** cinnamon 1002 **Iris** rainbow goddess 1003 **blow** bloom 1005 **purfl'd** embroidered 1006 **Elysian** Paradisal 1008-12 Adonis, a youth loved by Venus, goddess of love and Assyrian Queen because the Assyrians originated her worship and the story, was slain by a wild boar but, instead of being taken to the underworld, was carried by Venus to the beautiful Gardens of Adonis, the story being an allegory of the seasonal death and renewal of nature.

Where young *Adonis* oft reposes,
1010 Waxing well of his deep wound
In slumber soft, and on the ground
Sadly sits th' *Assyrian* Queen;
But farr above in spangled sheen
Celestial *Cupid* her fam'd Son advanc't,
Holds his dear *Psyche* sweet intranc't
After her wandring labours long,
Till free consent the gods among
Make her his eternal Bride,
And from her fair unspotted side
1020 Two blissful twins are to be born,
Youth and Joy; so *Jove* hath sworn.
    But now my task is smoothly don,
I can fly, or I can run
Quickly to the green earths end,
Where the bow'd welkin slow doth bend,
And from thence can soar as soon
To the corners of the Moon.
    Mortals that would follow me,
Love vertue, she alone is free,
1030 She can teach ye how to clime
Higher then the Spheary chime;
Or if Vertue feeble were,
Heav'n it self would stoop to her.

1013 **spangled sheen** star-spangled radiance 1013-20 **Cupid**,
son of Venus, and here celestial or heavenly rather than earthly
love, was much thwarted in his love for Psyche, representing the
human soul, upon whom the gods imposed many purifying
wanderings and labors before they permitted her union with her
lover. 1014 **advanc't** exalted in honour 1025 **welkin** sky
1031 **Spheary chime** see "Christ's Nativity" 125

SAMSON AGONISTES

A DRAMATIC POEM

Of that sort of Dramatic Poem which is call'd Tragedy.

TRAGEDY, as it was antiently compos'd, hath been ever held the gravest, moralest, and most profitable of all other Poems: therefore said by *Aristotle* to be of power by raising pity and fear, or terror, to purge the mind of those and such like passions, that is to temper and reduce them to just measure with a kind of delight, stirr'd up by reading or seeing those passions well imitated. Nor is Nature wanting in her own effects to make good his assertion: for so in Physic things of melancholic hue and quality are us'd against melancholy, sowr against sowr, salt to remove salt humours. Hence Philosophers and other gravest Writers, as *Cicero*, *Plutarch* and others, frequently cite out of Tragic Poets, both to adorn and illustrate thir discourse. The Apostle *Paul* himself thought it not unworthy to insert a verse of *Euripides* into the Text of Holy Scripture, 1 Cor. 15. 33. and *Paræus* commenting on the *Revelation,* divides the whole Book as a Tragedy, into Acts distinguisht each by a Chorus of Heavenly Harpings and Song between. Heretofore Men in highest dignity have labour'd not a little to be thought able to compose a Tragedy. Of that honour *Dionysius* the elder was no less ambitious, then before of his attaining to the Tyranny. *Augustus Cæsar* also had begun his *Ajax,* but unable to please his own judgment with what he had begun, left it unfinisht. *Seneca* the Philosopher is by some thought the Author of those Tragedies (at lest the best of them) that go under that name. *Gregory Nazianzen* a Father of the Church, thought it not unbeseeming the sanctity of his person to write a Tragedy, which he entitl'd, *Christ Suffering.* This is mention'd to vindicate Tragedy from the small esteem, or rather infamy, which in the account of many it undergoes at this day with other common Interludes; hap'ning through the Poets error of intermixing Comic stuff with Tragic sadness and gravity; or introducing trivial and vulgar persons, which by all judicious hath bin counted absurd; and brought in without discretion, corruptly to gratifie the people. And though antient Tragedy use no Prologue, yet using sometimes, in case of self defence, or explanation, that which *Martial* calls an Epistle; in behalf of this Tragedy coming forth after the antient manner, much different from what among us passes for best, thus much before-hand may be Epistl'd; that *Chorus* is here introduc'd after the Greek manner, not antient only but modern, and still in use among the *Italians*. In the modelling therefore of this Poem, with good reason, the Antients and *Italians* are rather follow'd, as of much more authority and fame. The measure of Verse us'd in the Chorus is of all sorts, call'd by the Greeks *Monostrophic*, or rather *Apolelymenon*, without regard had to *Strophe, Antistrophe* or *Epod*, which were a kind of Stanza's fram'd only for the Music, then us'd with the Chorus that sung; not essential to the Poem, and therefore not material; or being divided into Stanza's or Pauses, they may be call'd *Allæostropha*. Division into Act and Scene referring chiefly to the Stage (to which this work never was intended) is here omitted.

It suffices if the whole Drama be found not produc't beyond the fift Act, of the style and uniformitie, and that commonly call'd the Plot, whether intricate or explicit, which is nothing indeed but such œconomy, or disposition of the fable as may stand best with verisimilitude and decorum; they only will best judge who are not unacquainted with *Æschulus, Sophocles,* and *Euripides,* the three Tragic Poets unequall'd yet by any, and the best rule to all who endeavour to write Tragedy. The circumscription of time wherein the whole Drama begins and ends, is according to antient rule, and best example, within the space of 24 hours.

THE ARGUMENT

Samson *made Captive, Blind, and now in the Prison at* Gaza, *there to labour as in a common workhouse, on a Festival day, in the general cessation from labour, comes forth into the open Air, to a place nigh, somewhat retir'd there to sit a while and bemoan his condition. Where he happens at length to be visited by certain friends and equals of his tribe, which make the Chorus, who seek to comfort him what they can; then by his old Father Manoa, who endeavours the like, and withal tells him his purpose to procure his liberty by ransom; lastly, that this Feast was proclaim'd by the* Philistins *as a day of Thanksgiving for thir deliver-*

ance from the hands of Samson, *which yet more troubles him.* Manoa *then departs to prosecute his endeavour with the* Philistian *Lords for* Samson's *redemption; who in the mean while is visited by other persons; and lastly by a publick Officer to require his coming to the Feast before the Lords and People, to play or shew his strength in thir presence; he at first refuses, dismissing the publick Officer with absolute denyal to come; at length perswaded inwardly that this was from God, he yields to go along with him, who came now the second time with great threatnings to fetch him; the Chorus yet remaining on the place,* Manoa *returns full of joyful hope, to procure e're long his Sons deliverance: in the midst of which discourse an Ebrew comes in haste confusedly at first; and afterward more distinctly relating the Catastrophe, what* Samson *had done to the* Philistins, *and by accident to himself; wherewith the Tragedy ends.*

THE PERSONS.

SAMSON.	PUBLICK OFFICER.
MANOA *the Father of* SAMSON.	MESSENGER.
DALILA *his Wife.*	CHORUS OF DANITES.
HARAPHA OF GATH.	

The Scene before the Prison in Gaza.

is S. tragic hero ?
elemts of Gr tragedy
chorus acting part of drama (unlike Gr.)

Samson Agonistes

SAMS. A LITTLE onward lend thy guiding hand
To these dark steps, a little further on;
For yonder bank hath choice of Sun or shade,
There I am wont to sit, when any chance

Samson For the story of Samson see Judges XII-XVI **Agonistes,** the Greek word for an athlete competing for a prize in the public games, obviously refers to Samson's feats of strength at the festival of Dagon where his story ends; but the word also had for Milton and his contemporaries spiritual connotations. It suggested the spiritual as well as physical agony or struggle of Christ and of every Christian, Samson being regarded, like so many Old Testament figures, as a prefiguring of Christ and a type of the Christian. The word therefore also refers to the spiritual struggle within Samson which is the subject of Milton's drama and whose conclusion makes possible the final feats. Text from 1671 **11 day-spring** dawn

Relieves me from my task of servile toyl,
Daily in the common Prison else enjoyn'd me,
Where I a Prisoner chain'd, scarce freely draw
The air imprison'd also, close and damp,
Unwholsom draught: but here I feel amends,
10 The breath of Heav'n fresh-blowing, pure and sweet.
With day-spring born; here leave me to respire.
This day a solemn Feast the people hold
To *Dagon* thir Sea-Idol, and forbid
Laborious works, unwillingly this rest
Thir Superstition yields me; hence with leave
Retiring from the popular noise, I seek
This unfrequented place to find some ease,
Ease to the body some, none to the mind
From restless thoughts, that like a deadly swarm
20 Of Hornets arm'd, no sooner found alone,
But rush upon me thronging, and present
Times past, what once I was, and what am now.
O wherefore was my birth from Heaven foretold
Twice by an Angel, who at last in sight
Of both my Parents all in flames ascended
From off the Altar, where an Off'ring burn'd,
As in a fiery column charioting
His Godlike presence, and from some great act
Or benefit reveal'd to *Abraham*'s race?
30 Why was my breeding order'd and prescrib'd
As of a person separate to God,
Design'd for great exploits; if I must dye
Betray'd, Captiv'd, and both my Eyes put out,
Made of my Enemies the scorn and gaze;
To grind in Brazen Fetters under task
With this Heav'n-gifted strength? O glorious strength
Put to the labour of a Beast, debas't
Lower then bondslave! Promise was that I
Should *Israel* from *Philistian* yoke deliver;
40 Ask for this great Deliverer now, and find him
Eyeless in *Gaza* at the Mill with slaves,
Himself in bonds under *Philistian* yoke;

13 **Dagon** national God of the Philistines, half man, half fish
16 **popular** of the common people 31 **separate** set apart for,
Samson being a Nazarite, one who had taken special vows of
temperance and holiness 41 **Gaza** one of the chief Philistian
cities

Yet stay, let me not rashly call in doubt
Divine Prediction; what if all foretold
Had been fulfilld but through mine own default,
Whom have I to complain of but my self?
Who this high gift of strength committed to me,
In what part lodg'd, how easily bereft me,
Under the Seal of silence could not keep,
But weakly to a woman must reveal it,   50
O'recome with importunity and tears.
O impotence of mind, in body strong!
But what is strength without a double share
Of wisdom, vast, unwieldy, burdensom,
Proudly secure, yet liable to fall
By weakest suttleties, not made to rule,
But to subserve where wisdom bears command.
God, when he gave me strength, to shew withal
How slight the gift was, hung it in my Hair.
But peace, I must not quarrel with the will   60
Of highest dispensation, which herein
Happ'ly had ends above my reach to know:
Suffices that to me strength is my bane,
And proves the sourse of all my miseries;
So many, and so huge, that each apart
Would ask a life to wail, but chief of all,
O loss of sight, of thee I most complain!
Blind among enemies, O worse then chains,
Dungeon, or beggery, or decrepit age!
Light the prime work of God to me is extinct,   70
And all her various objects of delight
Annull'd, which might in part my grief have eas'd,
Inferiour to the vilest now become
Of man or worm; the vilest here excel me,
They creep, yet see, I dark in light expos'd
To daily fraud, contempt, abuse and wrong,
Within doors, or without, still as a fool,
In power of others, never in my own;
Scarce half I seem to live, dead more then half.
O dark, dark, dark, amid the blaze of noon,   80
Irrecoverably dark, total Eclipse
Without all hope of day!
O first created Beam, and thou great Word,
Let there be light, and light was over all;

55 **secure** careless 77 **still** always

Why am I thus bereav'd thy prime decree?
The Sun to me is dark
And silent as the Moon,
When she deserts the night
Hid in her vacant interlunar cave.
90 Since light so necessary is to life,
And almost life it self, if it be true
That light is in the Soul,
She all in every part; why was the sight
To such a tender ball as th' eye confin'd?
So obvious and so easie to be quench't,
And not as feeling through all parts diffus'd.
That she might look at will through every pore?
Then had I not been thus exil'd from light;
As in the land of darkness yet in light,
100 To live a life half dead, a living death,
And buried; but O yet more miserable!
My self, my Sepulcher, a moving Grave,
Buried, yet not exempt
By priviledge of death and burial
From worst of other evils, pains and wrongs,
But made hereby obnoxious more
To all the miseries of life,
Life in captivity
Among inhuman foes.
110 But who are these? for with joint pace I hear
The tread of many feet stearing this way;
Perhaps my enemies who come to stare
At my affliction, and perhaps to insult,
Thir daily practice to afflict me more.
      CHOR. This, this is he; softly a while,
Let us not break in upon him;
O change beyond report, thought, or belief!
See how he lies at random, carelessly diffus'd,
With languish't head unpropt,
120 As one past hope, abandon'd,
And by himself given over;
In slavish habit, ill-fitted weeds
O're worn and soild;
Or do my eyes misrepresent? Can this be hee,

89 **vacant** inactive **interlunar** between the waning of the old and
rising of the new moon 106 **obnoxious** exposed 118 **diffus'd**
stretched out 122 **habit** dress **weeds** clothing

That Heroic, that Renown'd,
Irresistible *Samson?* whom unarm'd
No strength of man, or fiercest wild beast could withstand;
Who tore the Lion, as the Lion tears the Kid,
Ran on embattelld Armies clad in Iron,
And weaponless himself,　　130
Made Arms ridiculous, useless the forgery
Of brazen shield and spear, the hammer'd Cuirass,
Chalybean temper'd steel, and frock of mail
Adamantean Proof;
But safest he who stood aloof,
When insupportably his foot advanc't,
In scorn of thir proud arms and warlike tools,
Spurn'd them to death by Troops. The bold *Ascalonite*
Fled from his Lion ramp, old Warriors turn'd
Thir plated backs under his heel;　　140
Or grovling soild thir crested helmets in the dust.
Then with what trivial weapon came to hand,
The Jaw of a dead Ass, his sword of bone,
A thousand fore-skins fell, the flower of *Palestin*
In *Ramath-lechi* famous to this day:
Then by main force pull'd up, and on his shoulders bore
The Gates of *Azza*, Post, and massie Bar
Up to the Hill by *Hebron*, seat of Giants old,
No journey of a Sabbath day, and loaded so;
Like whom the Gentiles feign to bear up Heav'n.　　150
Which shall I first bewail,
Thy Bondage or lost Sight,
Prison within Prison
Inseparably dark?
Thou art become (O worst imprisonment!)
The Dungeon of thy self; thy Soul
(Which Men enjoying sight oft without cause complain)
Imprison'd now indeed,

131 **forgery** process of making 133 **Chalybean** made by the
Chalybes of Pontus, famed for their ironwork 134 **Adamantean
proof** proof against diamond-hard steel 136 **insupportably** ir-
resistably 136 **Ascalonite** citizen of Ascalon, Philistian city
139 **Lion ramp** lion-like spring 144 **Palestin** Philistia 145 **Ra-
math-lechi** place of the lifting up of the jawbone 147 **Assa** Gaza
148 **Hebron** city forty miles from Gaza 149 **No . . . day** the
Mosaic Law limiting journeying on the Sabbath to less than a
mile 150 **whom** Atlas

In real darkness of the body dwells,
160 Shut up from outward light
To incorporate with gloomy night;
For inward light alas
Puts forth no visual beam.
O mirror of our fickle state,
Since man on earth unparallel'd?
The rarer thy example stands,
By how much from the top of wondrous glory,
Strongest of mortal men,
To lowest pitch of abject fortune thou art fall'n.
170 For him I reckon not in high estate
Whom long descent of birth
Or the sphear of fortune raises;
But thee whose strength, while vertue was her mate,
Might have subdu'd the Earth,
Universally crown'd with highest praises.

    SAM. I hear the sound of words, thir sense the air
Dissolves unjointed e're it reach my ear.

    CHOR. Hee speaks, let us draw nigh. Matchless in might,
The glory late of *Israel*, now the grief;
180 We come thy friends and neighbours not unknown
From *Eshtaol* and *Zora*'s fruitful Vale
To visit or bewail thee, or if better,
Counsel or Consolation we may bring,
Salve to thy Sores, apt words have power to swage
The tumors of a troubl'd mind,
And are as Balm to fester'd wounds.

    SAM. Your coming, Friends, revives me, for I learn
Now of my own experience, not by talk,
How counterfeit a coin they are who friends
190 Bear in their Superscription (of the most
I would be understood) in prosperous days
They swarm, but in adverse withdraw their head
Not to be found, though sought. Yee see, O friends,
How many evils have enclos'd me round;
Yet that which was the worst now least afflicts me,
Blindness, for had I sight. confus'd with shame,
How could I once look up, or heave the head,
Who like a foolish Pilot have shipwrack't,

163 **visual** sight-giving 172 **sphear** wheel 181 **Eshtaol, Zora**
Israelite cities 184 **swage** assuage 190 **Superscription** value
stamped on a coin

My Vessel trusted to me from above,
Gloriously rigg'd; and for a word, a tear,
Fool, have divulg'd the secret gift of God
To a deceitful Woman; tell me Friends, 200
Am I not sung and proverbd for a Fool
In every street, do they not say, how well
Are come upon him his deserts? yet why?
Immeasurable strength they might behold
In me, of wisdom nothing more then mean;
This with the other should, at least, have paird,
These two proportiond ill drove me transverse.

   CHOR. Tax not divine disposal, wisest Men 210
Have err'd, and by bad Women been deceiv'd;
And shall again, pretend they ne're so wise.
Deject not then so overmuch thy self,
Who hast of sorrow thy full load besides;
Yet truth to say, I oft have heard men wonder
Why thou shouldst wed *Philistian* women rather
Then of thine own Tribe fairer, or as fair,
At least of thy own Nation, and as noble.

   SAM. The first I saw at *Timna*, and she pleas'd
Mee, not my Parents, that I sought to wed, 220
The daughter of an Infidel: they knew not
That what I motion'd was of God; I knew
From intimate impulse, and therefore urg'd
The Marriage on; that by occasion hence
I might begin *Israel*'s Deliverance,
The work to which I was divinely call'd;
She proving false, the next I took to Wife
(O that I never had! fond wish too late)
Was in the Vale of *Sorec, Dalila,*
That specious Monster, my accomplisht snare. 230
I thought it lawful from my former act,
And the same end; still watching to oppress
Israel's oppressours: of what now I suffer
She was not the prime cause, but I my self,
Who vanquisht with a peal of words (O weakness!)
Gave up my fort of silence to a Woman.

   CHOR. In seeking just occasion to provoke
The *Philistine*, thy Countries Enemy,

207 **mean** middling, average 208 **paird** been equal 209 **transverse** off the straight line 210 **tax** blame 219 **Timna** Philistian city 223 **intimate** inward

Thou never wast remiss, I bear thee witness:
240 Yet *Israel* still serves with all his Sons.
    SAM. That fault I take not on me, but transfer
On *Israel's* Governours, and Heads of Tribes,
Who seeing those great acts which God had done
Singly by me against their Conquerours
Acknowledg'd not, or not at all consider'd
Deliverance offerd: I on th' other side
Us'd no ambition to commend my deeds,
The deeds themselves, though mute, spoke loud the dooer;
But they persisted deaf, and would not seem
250 To count them things worth notice, till at length
Thir Lords the *Philistines* with gather'd powers
Enterd *Judea* seeking mee, who then
Safe to the rock of *Etham* was retir'd,
Not flying, but fore-casting in what place
To set upon them, what advantag'd best;
Mean while the men of *Judah* to prevent
The harass of thir Land, beset me round;
I willingly on some conditions came
Into thir hands, and they as gladly yield me
260 To the uncircumcis'd a welcom prey,
Bound with two cords; but cords to me were threds
Toucht with the flame: on thir whole Host I flew
Unarm'd, and with a trivial weapon fell'd
Their choicest youth; they only liv'd who fled.
Had *Judah* that day join'd, or one whole Tribe,
They had by this possess'd the Towers of *Gath*,
And lorded over them whom now they serve;
But what more oft in Nations grown corrupt,
And by thir vices brought to servitude,
270 Then to love Bondage more than Liberty,
Bondage with ease then strenuous liberty;
And to despise, or envy, or suspect
Whom God hath of his special favour rais'd
As thir Deliverer; if he aught begin,
How frequent to desert him, and at last
To heap ingratitude on worthiest deeds?
    CHOR. Thy words to my remembrance bring
How *Succoth* and the Fort of *Penuel*
Thir great Deliverer contemn'd,
280 The matchless *Gideon* in pursuit

278-81 Judges VIII: 4-9

Of *Madian* and her vanquisht Kings:
And how ingrateful *Ephraim*
Had dealt with *Jephtha*, who by argument,
Not worse then by his shield and spear
Defended *Israel* from the *Ammonite*,
Had not his prowess quell'd thir pride
In that sore battel when so many dy'd
Without Reprieve adjudg'd to death,
For want of well pronouncing *Shibboleth*.

SAM. Of such examples adde mee to the roul,   290
Mee easily indeed mine may neglect,
But Gods propos'd deliverance not so.
CHOR. Just are the ways of God,
And justifiable to Men;
Unless there be who think not God at all,
If any be, they walk obscure;
For of such Doctrine never was there School,
But the heart of the Fool,
And no man therein Doctor but himself.

Yet more there be who doubt his ways not just,   300
As to his own edicts, found contradicting,
Then give the rains to wandring thought,
Regardless of his glories diminution;
Till by thir own perplexities involv'd
They ravel more, still less resolv'd,
But never find self-satisfying solution.

As if they would confine th' interminable,
And tie him to his own prescript,
Who made our Laws to bind us, not himself,
And hath full right to exempt   310
Whom so it pleases him by choice
From National obstriction, without taint
Of sin, or legal debt;
For with his own Laws he can best dispence.
He would not else who never wanted means,
Nor in respect of the enemy just cause
To set his people free,
Have prompted this Heroic *Nazarite*,

282-9 Judges XII: 5-6 291 **mine** my people 295 **think not** think
there is no 296 **obscure** in darkness 299 **Doctor** teacher
305 **ravel** entangle **still** always 307 **interminable** without limit,
infinite 312 **obstriction** obligation, here the Mosaic law against
marriage with Gentiles 318 **Nazarite** see above 31

Against his vow of strictest purity,
320 To seek in marriage that fallacious Bride,
Unclean, unchaste.
    Down Reason then, at least vain reasonings **down,**
Though Reason here aver
That moral verdit quits her of unclean:
Unchaste was subsequent, her stain not his.
    But see here comes thy reverend Sire
With careful step, Locks white as doune,
Old *Manoah:* advise
Forthwith how thou oughtst to receive him.
330   SAM. Ay me, another inward grief awak't,
With mention of that name renews th' assault.
    MAN. Brethren and men of *Dan,* for such ye seem,
Though in this uncouth place; if old respect,
As I suppose, towards your once gloried friend,
My Son now Captive, hither hath inform'd
Your younger feet, while mine cast back with age
Came lagging after; say if he be here.
    CHOR. As signal now in low dejected state,
As earst in highest, behold him where he lies.
340   MAN. O miserable change! is this the man,
That invincible *Samson,* far renown'd,
The dread of *Israel's* foes, who with a strength
Equivalent to Angels walk'd thir streets,
None offering fight; who single combatant
Duell'd thir Armies rank't in proud array,
Himself an Army, now unequal match
To save himself against a coward arm'd
At one spears length. O ever failing trust
In mortal strength! and oh what not in man
350 Deceivable and vain! Nay what thing good
Pray'd for, but often proves our woe, our bane?
I pray'd for Children, and thought barrenness
In wedlock a reproach; I gain'd a Son,
And such a Son as all Men hail'd me happy;
Who would be now a Father in my stead?
O wherefore did God grant me my request,
And as a blessing with such pomp adorn'd?
Why are his gifts desirable, to tempt
Our earnest Prayers, then giv'n with solemn hand

333 **uncouth** unfamiliar 335 **inform'd** guided 338 **signal** conspicuous

As Graces, draw a Scorpions tail behind? 360
For this did the Angel twice descend? for this
Ordain'd thy nurture holy, as of a Plant;
Select, and Sacred, Glorious for a while,
The miracle of men: then in an hour
Ensnar'd, assaulted, overcome, led bound,
Thy Foes derision, Captive, Poor, and Blind
Into a Dungeon thrust, to work with Slaves?
Alas methinks whom God hath chosen once
To worthiest deeds, if he through frailty err,
He should not so o'rewhelm, and as a thrall 370
Subject him to so foul indignities,
Be it but for honours sake of former deeds.

questiong God

SAM. Appoint not heavenly disposition, Father,
Nothing of all these evils hath befall'n me
But justly; I my self have brought them on,

S defends God, blames Self

Sole Author I, sole cause: if aught seem vile,
As vile hath been my folly, who have profan'd
The mystery of God giv'n me under pledge
Of vow, and have betray'd it to a woman,
A *Canaanite,* my faithless enemy. 380
This well I knew, nor was at all surpris'd,
But warn'd by oft experience: did not she
Of *Timna* first betray me, and reveal
The secret wrested from me in her highth
Of Nuptial Love profest, carrying it strait
To them who had corrupted her, my Spies,
And Rivals? In this other was there found
More Faith? who also in her prime of love,
Spousal embraces, vitiated with Gold,
Though offer'd only, by the sent conceiv'd 390
Her spurious first-born; Treason against me?
Thrice she assay'd with flattering prayers and sighs,
And amorous reproaches to win from me
My capital secret, in what part my strength
Lay stor'd, in what part summ'd, that she might know;
Thrice I deluded her, and turn'd to sport
Her importunity, each time perceiving
How openly, and with what impudence
She purpos'd to betray me, and (which was worse
Then undissembl'd hate) with what contempt 400
She sought to make me Traytor to my self;
Yet the fourth time, when mustring all her wiles,

With blandisht parlies, feminine assaults,
Tongue-batteries, she surceas'd not day nor night
To storm me over-watch't, and wearied out.
At times when men seek most repose and rest,
I yielded, and unlock'd her all my heart,
Who with a grain of manhood well resolv'd
Might easily have shook off all her snares:
410 But foul effeminacy held me yok't
Her Bond-slave; O indignity, O blot
To Honour and Religion! servil mind
Rewarded well with servil punishment!
The base degree to which I now am fall'n,
These rags, this grinding, is not yet so base
As was my former servitude, ignoble,
Unmanly, ignominious, infamous,
True slavery, and that blindness worse then this,
That saw not how degeneratly I serv'd.
420 　MAN. I cannot praise thy Marriage choises, Son,
Rather approv'd them not; but thou didst plead
Divine impulsion prompting how thou might'st
Find some occasion to infest our Foes.
I state not that; this I am sure; our Foes
Found soon occasion thereby to make thee
Thir Captive, and thir triumph; thou the sooner
Temptation found'st, or over-potent charms
To violate the sacred trust of silence
Deposited within thee; which to have kept
430 Tacit, was in thy power; true; and thou bear'st
Enough, and more the burden of that fault;
Bitterly hast thou paid, and still art paying
That rigid score. A worse thing yet remains,
This day the *Philistines* a popular Feast
Here celebrate in *Gaza;* and proclaim
Great Pomp, and Sacrifice, and Praises loud
To *Dagon,* as their God who hath deliver'd
Thee *Samson* bound and blind into thir hands,
Them out of thine, who slew'st them many a slain.
440 So *Dagon* shall be magnifi'd, and God,
Besides whom is no God, compar'd with Idols,
Disglorifi'd, blasphem'd, and had in scorn
By th' Idolatrous rout amidst thir wine;

423 **infest** harass　424 **state not** do not enter into the details of
430 **tacit** hidden in silence　433 **score** debt

Which to have come to pass by means of thee,
Samson, of all thy sufferings think the heaviest,
Of all reproach the most with shame that ever
Could have befall'n thee and thy Fathers house.

SAM. Father, I do acknowledge and confess
That I this honour, I this pomp have brought
To *Dagon,* and advanc'd his praises high   450
Among the Heathen round; to God have brought
Dishonour, obloquie, and op't the mouths
Of Idolists, and Atheists; have brought scandal
To *Israel,* diffidence of God, and doubt
In feeble hearts, propense anough before
To waver, or fall off and joyn with Idols;
Which is my chief affliction, shame and sorrow,
The anguish of my Soul, that suffers not
Mine eie to harbour sleep, or thoughts to rest.
This only hope relieves me, that the strife   460
With me hath end; all the contest is now
'Twixt God and *Dagon; Dagon* hath presum'd,
Me overthrown, to enter lists with God,
His Deity comparing and preferring
Before the God of *Abraham.* He, be sure,
Will not connive, or linger, thus provok'd,
But will arise and his great name assert:
Dagon must stoop, and shall e're long receive
Such a discomfit, as shall quite despoil him
Of all these boasted Trophies won on me,   470
And with confusion blank his Worshippers.

MAN. With cause this hope relieves thee, and these words
I as a Prophecy receive: for God,
Nothing more certain, will not long defer
To vindicate the glory of his name
Against all competition, nor will long
Endure it, doubtful whether God be Lord,
Or *Dagon.* But for the what shall be done?
Thou must not in the mean while here forgot
Lie in this miserable loathsom plight   480
Neglected. I already have made way
To some *Philistian* Lords, with whom to treat
About thy ransom: well they may by this
Have satisfi'd thir utmost of revenge
By pains and slaveries, worse then death inflicted

454 **diffidence** distrust 455 **propense** inclined

On thee, who now no more canst do them harm.

SAM. Spare that proposal, Father, spare the trouble
Of that sollicitation; let me here,
As I deserve, pay on my punishment;
490　And expiate, if possible, my crime,
Shameful garrulity. To have reveal'd
Secrets of men, the secrets of a friend,
How hainous had the fact been, how deserving
Contempt, and scorn of all, to be excluded
All friendship, and avoided as a blab,
The mark of fool set on his front?
But I Gods counsel have not kept, his holy secret
Presumptuously have publish'd, impiously,
Weakly at least, and shamefully: A sin
500　That Gentiles in thir Parables condemn
To thir abyss and horrid pains confin'd.

MAN. Be penitent and for thy fault contrite,
But act not in thy own affliction, Son,
Repent the sin, but if the punishment
Thou canst avoid, self-preservation bids;
Or th' execution leave to high disposal,
And let another hand, not thine, exact
Thy penal forfeit from thy self; perhaps
God will relent, and quit thee all his debt;
510　Who evermore approves and more accepts
(Best pleas'd with humble and filial submission)
Him who imploring mercy sues for life,
Then who self-rigorous chooses death as due;
Which argues over-just, and self-displeas'd
For self-offence, more then for God offended.
Reject not then what offerd means, who knows
But God hath set before us, to return thee
Home to thy countrey and his sacred house,
Where thou mayst bring thy off'rings, to avert
520　His further ire, with praiers and vows renew'd.

SAM. His pardon I implore; but as for life,
To what end should I seek it? when in strength
All mortals I excell'd, and great in hopes

489 **pay on** go on paying　493 **fact** deed　500-1 An allusion to the
story of Tantalus, punished for betraying the secrets of Zeus by
being immersed in water up to his neck beneath a fruit tree with-
out the power to drink or reach for food.　514 **over-just** exces-
sively severe

With youthful courage and magnanimous thoughts
Of birth from Heav'n foretold and high exploits,
Full of divine instinct, after some proof
Of acts indeed heroic, far beyond
The Sons of *Anac,* famous now and blaz'd,
Fearless of danger, like a petty God
I walk'd about admir'd of all and dreaded   530
On hostile ground, none daring my affront.
Then swoll'n with pride into the snare I fell
Of fair fallacious looks, venereal trains,
Softn'd with pleasure and voluptuous life;
At length to lay my head and hallow'd pledge
Of all my strength in the lascivious lap
Of a deceitful Concubine who shore me
Like a tame Weather, all my precious fleece,
Then turn'd me out ridiculous, despoil'd,
Shav'n, and disarm'd among my enemies.   540
    CHOR. Desire of wine and all delicious drinks,
Which many a famous Warriour overturns,
Thou couldst repress, nor did the dancing Rubie
Sparkling, out-pow'rd, the flavor, or the smell,
Or taste that cheers the heart of Gods and men,
Allure thee from the cool Crystalline stream.
    SAM. Where ever fountain or fresh current flow'd
Against the Eastern ray, translucent, pure,
With touch ætherial of Heav'ns fiery rod
I drank, from the clear milkie juice allaying   550
Thirst, and refresht; nor envy'd them the grape
Whose heads that turbulent liquor fills with fumes.
    CHOR. O madness, to think use of strongest wines
And strongest drinks our chief support of health,
When God with these forbid'n made choice to rear
His mighty Champion, strong above compare,
Whose drink was only from the liquid brook.
    SAM. But what avail'd this temperance, not compleat
Against another object more enticing?
What boots it at one gate to make defence,   560
And at another to let in the foe
Effeminatly vanquish't? by which means,
Now blind, disheartn'd, sham'd, dishonour'd, quell'd,

528 **Anac** a giant, Numbers XIII: 33 531 **my affront** to meet me
533 **venereal trains** love lures 547-8 Ezekiel XLVII 548 **against**
towards 549 **rod** sun's rays 560 **boots it** good does it do

To what can I be useful, wherein serve
My Nation, and the work from Heav'n impos'd,
But to sit idle on the houshold hearth,
A burdenous drone; to visitants a gaze,
Or pitied object, these redundant locks
Robustious to no purpose clustring down,
570 Vain monument of strength; till length of years
And sedentary numness craze my limbs
To a contemptible old age obscure.
Here rather let me drudge and earn my bread,
Till vermin or the draff of servil food
Consume me, and oft-invocated death
Hast'n the welcom end of all my pains.
    Man. Wilt thou then serve the *Philistines* with that gift
Which was expresly giv'n thee to annoy them?
Better at home lie bed-rid, not only idle,
580 Inglorious, unimploy'd, with age out-worn.
But God who caus'd a fountain at thy prayer
From the dry ground to spring, thy thirst to allay
After the brunt of battel, can as easie
Cause light again within thy eies to spring,
Wherewith to serve him better then thou hast;
And I perswade me so; why else this strength
Miraculous yet remaining in those locks?
His might continues in thee not for naught,
Nor shall his wondrous gifts be frustrate thus.
590   Sam. All otherwise to me my thoughts portend,
That these dark orbs no more shall treat with light,
Nor th' other light of life continue long,
But yield to double darkness nigh at hand:
So much I feel my genial spirits droop,
My hopes all flat, nature within me seems
In all her functions weary of herself;
My race of glory run, and race of shame,
And I shall shortly be with them that rest.
    Man. Believe not these suggestions which proceed
600 From anguish of the mind and humours black,
That mingle with thy fancy. I however
Must not omit a Fathers timely care
To prosecute the means of thy deliverance

568 **redundant** flowing 569 **Robustious** vigorous 571 **craze** impair 574 **draff** refuse 578 **annoy** damage 594 **genial spirits** spirits fundamental to a man's nature

By ransom or how else: mean while be calm,
And healing words from these thy friends admit.
  Sam. O that torment should not be confin'd
To the bodies wounds and sores
With maladies innumerable
In heart, head, brest, and reins;
But must secret passage find   610
To th' inmost mind,
There exercise all his fierce accidents,
And on her purest spirits prey,
As on entrails, joints, and limbs,
With answerable pains, but more intense,
Though void of corporal sense.
  My griefs not only pain me
As a lingring disease,
But finding no redress, ferment and rage,
Nor less then wounds immedicable   620
Ranckle, and fester, and gangrene,
To black mortification.
Thoughts my Tormentors arm'd with deadly stings
Mangle my apprehensive tenderest parts,
Exasperate, exulcerate, and raise
Dire inflammation which no cooling herb
Or medcinal liquor can asswage,
Nor breath of Vernal Air from snowy *Alp.*
Sleep hath forsook and giv'n me o're
To deaths benumming Opium as my only cure.   630
Thence faintings, swounings of despair,
And sense of Heav'ns desertion.
  I was his nursling once and choice delight,
His destin'd from the womb,
Promisd by Heavenly message twice descending.
Under his special eie
Abstemious I grew up and thriv'd amain;
He led me on to mightiest deeds
Above the nerve of mortal arm
Against the uncircumcis'd, our enemies.   640
But now hath cast me off as never known,
And to those cruel enemies,
Whom I by his appointment had provok't,
Left me all helpless with th' irreparable loss

609 **reins** loins 612 **accidents** symptoms 615 **answerable** corresponding 624 **apprehensive** sensitive 639 **nerve** sinew

Of sight, reserv'd alive to be repeated
The subject of thir cruelty, or scorn.
Nor am I in the list of them that hope;
Hopeless are all my evils, all remediless;
This one prayer yet remains, might I be heard,
650 No long petition, speedy death,
The close of all my miseries, and the balm.
   CHOR. Many are the sayings of the wise   *Stoics*
In antient and in modern books enroll'd;
Extolling Patience as the truest fortitude;
And to the bearing well of all calamities,
All chances incident to mans frail life
Consolatories writ
With studied argument, and much perswasion sought
Lenient of grief and anxious thought,
660 But with th' afflicted in his pangs thir sound
Little prevails, or rather seems a tune,
Harsh, and of dissonant mood from his complaint,
Unless he feel within
Some source of consolation from above;
Secret refreshings, that repair his strength,
And fainting spirits uphold.
   God of our Fathers, what is man!
That thou towards him with hand so various,
Or might I say contrarious,
670 Temperst thy providence through his short course,
Not evenly, as thou rul'st
The Angelic orders and inferiour creatures mute,
Irrational and brute.
Nor do I name of men the common rout,
That wandring loose about
Grow up and perish, as the summer flie,
Heads without name no more rememberd,
But such as thou hast solemnly elected,
With gifts and graces eminently adorn'd
680 To some great work, thy glory,
And peoples safety, which in part they effect:
Yet toward these thus dignifi'd, thou oft
Amidst thir highth of noon,
Changest thy countenance, and thy hand with no regard
Of highest favours past
From thee on them, or them to thee of service.

659 **Lenient of** softening

Nor only dost degrade them, or remit
To life obscur'd, which were a fair dismission,
But throw'st them lower then thou didst exalt them high,
Unseemly falls in human eie,   690
Too grievous for the trespass or omission,
Oft leav'st them to the hostile sword
Of Heathen and prophane, thir carkasses
To dogs and fowls a prey, or else captiv'd:
Or to the unjust tribunals, under change of times,
And condemnation of the ingrateful multitude.
If these they scape, perhaps in poverty
With sickness and disease thou bow'st them down,
Painful diseases and deform'd,
In crude old age;   700
Though not disordinate, yet causless suffring
The punishment of dissolute days, in fine,
Just or unjust, alike seem miserable,
For oft alike, both come to evil end.
   So deal not with this once thy glorious Champion,
The Image of thy strength, and mighty minister.
What do I beg? how hast thou dealt already?
Behold him in this state calamitous, and turn
His labours, for thou canst, to peaceful end.
   But who is this, what thing of Sea or Land?   710
Femal of sex it seems,
That so bedeckt, ornate, and gay,
Comes this way sailing
Like a stately Ship
Of *Tarsus,* bound for th' Isles
Of *Javan* or *Gadier*
With all her bravery on, and tackle trim,
Sails fill'd, and streamers waving,
Courted by all the winds that hold them play,
An Amber sent of odorous perfume   720
Her harbinger, a damsel train behind;
Some rich *Philistian* Matron she may seem,
And now at nearer view, no other certain
Then *Dalila* thy wife.
   SAM. My Wife, my Traytress, let her not come near me.

687 **remit** send back 700 **crude** premature 701 **disordinate** in-
temperate 706 **minister** servant 715 **Tarsus** city in Asia Minor
famed for its fleets 716 **Javan** Ionia **Gadier** Cadiz 717 **bravery**
finery 720 **Amber** ambergris 721 **harbinger** forerunner

CHOR. Yet on she moves, now stands & eies thee fixt,
About t' have spoke, but now, with head declin'd
Like a fair flower surcharg'd with dew, she weeps
And words addrest seem into tears dissolv'd,
730 Wetting the borders of her silk'n veil:
But now again she makes address to speak.

DAL. With doubtful feet and wavering resolution
I came, still dreading thy displeasure, *Samson,*
Which to have merited, without excuse,
I cannot but acknowledge; yet if tears
May expiate (though the fact more evil drew
In the perverse event then I foresaw)
My penance hath not slack'n'd, though my pardon
No way assur'd. But conjugal affection
740 Prevailing over fear, and timerous doubt
Hath led me on desirous to behold
Once more thy face, and know of thy estate.
If aught in my ability may serve
To light'n what thou suffer'st, and appease
Thy mind with what amends is in my power,
Though late, yet in some part to recompense
My rash but more unfortunate misdeed.

SAM. Out, out *Hyæna;* these are thy wonted arts,
And arts of every woman false like thee,
750 To break all faith, all vows, deceive, betray,
Then as repentant to submit, beseech,
And reconcilement move with feign'd remorse,
Confess, and promise wonders in her change,
Not truly penitent, but chief to try
Her husband, how far urg'd his patience bears,
His vertue or weakness which way to assail:
Then with more cautious and instructed skill
Again transgresses, and again submits;
That wisest and best men full oft beguil'd
760 With goodness principl'd not to reject
The penitent, but ever to forgive,
Are drawn to wear out miserable days,
Entangl'd with a poysnous bosom snake,
If not by quick destruction soon cut off

729 **addrest** prepared for speech 736 **fact** deed 737 **event** outcome 742 **estate** condition 748 **Hyaena** supposed to imitate the human voice to entrap men and devour them 752 **move** propose 760 **principl'd** instructed

As I by thee, to Ages an example.
   DAL. Yet hear me *Samson;* not that I endeavour
To lessen or extenuate my offence,
But that on th' other side if it be weigh'd
By it self, with aggravations not surcharg'd,
Or else with just allowance counterpois'd,   770
I may, if possible, thy pardon find
The easier towards me, or thy hatred less.
First granting, as I do, it was a weakness
In me, but incident to all our sex,
Curiosity, inquisitive, importune
Of secrets, then with like infirmity
To publish them, both common female faults:
Was it not weakness also to make known
For importunity, that is for naught,
Wherein consisted all thy strength and safety?   780
To what I did thou shewdst me first the way.
But I to enemies reveal'd, and should not.
Nor shouldst thou have trusted that to womans **frailty**
E're I to thee, thou to thy self wast cruel.
Let weakness then with weakness come to parl
So near related, or the same of kind,
Thine forgive mine; that men may censure thine
The gentler, if severely thou exact not
More strength from me, then in thy self was found.
And what if Love, which thou interpret'st hate,   790
The jealousie of Love, powerful of sway
In human hearts, nor less in mine towards thee,
Caus'd what I did? I saw thee mutable
Of fancy, feard lest one day thou wouldst leave me
As her at *Timna,* sought by all means therefore
How to endear, and hold thee to me firmest:
No better way I saw then by importuning
To learn thy secrets, get into my power
Thy key of strength and safety: thou wilt say,
Why then reveal'd? I was assur'd by those   800
Who tempted me, that nothing was design'd
Against thee but safe custody, and hold:
That made for me, I knew that liberty
Would draw thee forth to perilous enterprises,
While I at home sate full of cares and fears

785 **parl** parley 786 **kind** nature 794 **fancy** affection 803 **made
for me** was to my advantage

Wailing thy absence in my widow'd bed;
Here I should still enjoy thee day and night
Mine and Loves prisoner, not the *Philistines,*
Whole to my self, unhazarded abroad,
810 Fearless at home of partners in my love.
These reasons in Loves law have past for good,
Though fond and reasonless to some perhaps;
And Love hath oft, well meaning, wrought much wo
Yet always pity or pardon hath obtain'd.
Be not unlike all others, not austere
As thou art strong, inflexible as steel.
If thou in strength all mortals dost exceed,
In uncompassionate anger do not so.
    SAM. How cunningly the sorceress displays
820 Her own transgressions, to upbraid me mine?
That malice not repentance brought thee hither,
By this appears: I gave, thou say'st, th' example,
I led the way; bitter reproach, but true,
I to my self was false e're thou to me,
Such pardon therefore as I give my folly,
Take to thy wicked deed: which when thou seest
Impartial, self-severe, inexorable,
Thou wilt renounce thy seeking, and much rather
Confess it feign'd, weakness is thy excuse,
830 And I believe it, weakness to resist
Philistian gold: if weakness may excuse,
What Murtherer, what Traytor, Parricide,
Incestuous, Sacrilegious, but may plead it?
All wickedness is weakness: that plea therefore
With God or Man will gain thee no remission.
But Love constrain'd thee; call it furious rage
To satisfie thy lust: Love seeks to have Love;
My love how couldst thou hope, who tookst the way
To raise in me inexpiable hate,
840 Knowing, as needs I must, by thee betray'd?
In vain thou striv'st to cover shame with shame,
Or by evasions thy crime uncoverst more.
    DAL. Since thou determinst weakness for no plea
In man or woman, though to thy own condemning,
Hear what assaults I had, what snares besides,
What sieges girt me round, e're I consented;
Which might have aw'd the best resolv'd of men,
812 **fond** foolish

The constantest to have yielded without blame.
It was not gold, as to my charge thou lay'st,
That wrought with me: thou know'st the Magistrates   850
And Princes of my countrey came in person,
Sollicited, commanded, threatn'd, urg'd,
Adjur'd by all the bonds of civil Duty
And of Religion, press'd how just it was,
How honourable, how glorious to entrap
A common enemy, who had destroy'd
Such numbers of our Nation: and the Priest
Was not behind, but ever at my ear,
Preaching how meritorious with the gods
It would be to ensnare an irreligious   860
Dishonourer of *Dagon*: what had I
To oppose against such powerful arguments?
Only my love of thee held long debate;
And combated in silence all these reasons
With hard contest: at length that grounded maxim
So rife and celebrated in the mouths
Of wisest men, that to the public good
Private respects must yield, with grave authority
Took full possession of me and prevail'd;
Vertue, as I thought, truth, duty so enjoyning.   870
    SAM. I thought where all thy circling wiles would end;
In feign'd Religion, smooth hypocrisie.
But had thy love, still odiously pretended,
Bin, as it ought, sincere, it would have taught thee
Far other reasonings, brought forth other deeds.
I before all the daughters of my Tribe
And of my Nation chose thee from among
My enemies, lov'd thee, as too well thou knew'st,
Too well, unbosom'd all my secrets to thee,
Not out of levity, but over-powr'd   880
By thy request, who could deny thee nothing;
Yet now am judg'd an enemy. Why then
Didst thou at first receive me for thy husband?
Then, as since then, thy countries foe profest:
Being once a wife, for me thou wast to leave
Parents and countrey; nor was I their subject,
Nor under their protection but my own,
Thou mine, not theirs: if aught against my life
Thy countrey sought of thee, it sought unjustly,

868 **respects** considerations

890 Against the law of nature, law of nations,
No more thy countrey, but an impious crew
Of men conspiring to uphold thir state
By worse then hostile deeds, violating the ends
For which our countrey is a name so dear;
Not therefore to be obey'd. But zeal mov'd thee;
To please thy gods thou didst it; gods unable
To acquit themselves and prosecute their foes
But by ungodly deeds, the contradiction
Of their own deity, Gods cannot be:
900 Less therefore to be pleas'd, obey'd, or fear'd,
These false pretexts and varnish'd colours failing,
Bare in thy guilt how foul must thou appear?
    DAL. In argument with men a woman ever
Goes by the worse, whatever be her cause.
    SAM. For want of words no doubt, or lack of breath,
Witness when I was worried with thy peals.
    DAL. I was a fool, too rash, and quite mistaken
In what I thought would have succeeded best.
Let me obtain forgiveness of thee, *Samson*,
910 Afford me place to shew what recompence
Towards thee I intend for what I have misdone,
Misguided; only what remains past cure
Bear not too sensibly, nor still insist
To afflict thy self in vain: though sight be lost,
Life yet hath many solaces, enjoy'd
Where other senses want not their delights
At home in leisure and domestic ease,
Exempt from many a care and chance to which
Eye-sight exposes daily men abroad.
920 I to the Lords will intercede, not doubting
Thir favourable ear, that I may fetch thee
From forth this loathsom prison-house, to abide
With me, where my redoubl'd love and care
With nursing diligence, to me glad office,
May ever tend about thee to old age
With all things grateful chear'd, and so suppli'd,
That what by me thou hast lost thou least shalt miss.
    SAM. No, no, of my condition take no care;
It fits not; thou and I long since are twain;
930 Nor think me so unwary or accurst

904 **goes by** gets 913 **sensibly** sensitively 919 **abroad out of
doors** 924 **office** duty 926 **grateful** comforting

To bring my feet again into the snare
Where once I have been caught; I know thy trains
Though dearly to my cost, thy ginns, and toyls;
Thy fair enchanted cup, and warbling charms
No more on me have power, their force is null'd,
So much of Adders wisdom I have learn't
To fence my ear against thy sorceries.
If in my flower of youth and strength, when all men
Lov'd, honour'd, fear'd me, thou alone could hate me
Thy Husband, slight me, sell me, and forgo me;   940
How wouldst thou use me now, blind, and thereby
Deceiveable, in most things as a child
Helpless, thence easily contemn'd, and scorn'd,
And last neglected? How wouldst thou insult
When I must live uxorious to thy will
In perfect thraldom, how again betray me,
Bearing my words and doings to the Lords
To gloss upon, and censuring, frown or smile?
This Gaol I count the house of Liberty
To thine whose doors my feet shall never enter.   950
   DAL. Let me approach at least, and touch thy hand.
   SAM. Not for thy life, lest fierce remembrance wake
My sudden rage to tear thee joint by joint.
At distance I forgive thee, go with that;
Bewail thy falshood, and the pious works
It hath brought forth to make thee memorable
Among illustrious women, faithful wives:
Cherish thy hast'n'd widowhood with the gold
Of Matrimonial treason: so farewel.
   DAL. I see thou art implacable, more deaf   960
To prayers, then winds and seas, yet winds to seas
Are reconcil'd at length, and Sea to Shore:
Thy anger, unappeasable, still rages,
Eternal tempest never to be calm'd.
Why do I humble thus my self, and suing
For peace, reap nothing but repulse and hate?
Bid go with evil omen and the brand
Of infamy upon my name denounc't?
To mix with thy concernments I desist
Henceforth, nor too much disapprove my own.   970
Fame if not double-fac't is double-mouth'd,

932 **trains** lures 933 **ginns** snares **toyls** nets 936 Psalms **LIX: 4-5**,
adders being supposedly deaf 948 **gloss** comment

And with contrary blast proclaims most deeds,
On both his wings, one black, th' other white,
Bears greatest names in his wild aerie flight.
My name perhaps among the Circumcis'd
In *Dan,* in *Judah,* and the bordering Tribes,
To all posterity may stand defam'd,
With malediction mention'd, and the blot
Of falshood most unconjugal traduc't.
980 But in my countrey where I most desire,
In *Ecron, Gaza, Asdod,* and in *Gath*
I shall be nam'd among the famousest
Of Women, sung at solemn festivals,
Living and dead recorded, who to save
Her countrey from a fierce destroyer, chose
Above the faith of wedlock-bands, my tomb
With odours visited and annual flowers.
Not less renown'd then in Mount *Ephraim,*
Jael, who with inhospitable guile
990 Smote *Sisera* sleeping through the Temples nail'd.
Nor shall I count it hainous to enjoy
The public marks of honour and reward
Conferr'd upon me, for the piety
Which to my countrey I was judg'd to have shewn.
At this who ever envies or repines
I leave him to his lot, and like my own.
     CHOR. She's gone, a manifest Serpent by her sting
Discover'd in the end, till now conceal'd.
     SAM. So let her go, God sent her to debase me,
1000 And aggravate my folly who committed
To such a viper his most sacred trust
Of secresie, my safety, and my life.
     CHOR. Yet beauty, though injurious, hath strange power,
After offence returning, to regain
Love once possest, nor can be easily
Repuls't, without much inward passion felt
And secret sting of amorous remorse.
     SAM. Love-quarrels oft in pleasing concord end,
Not wedlock-trechery endangering life.
1010   CHOR. It is not vertue, wisdom, valour, wit,
Strength, comliness of shape, or amplest merit
That womans love can win or long inherit;

988-90 Judges IV: 17-21   1000 **aggravate** emphasize or make
heavy 1012 **inherit** possess

But what it is, hard is to say,
Harder to hit,
(Which way soever men refer it)
Much like thy riddle, *Samson*, in one day
Or seven, though one should musing sit;
 If any of these or all, the *Timnian* bride
Had not so soon preferr'd
Thy Paranymph, worthless to thee compar'd,   1020
Successour in thy bed,
Nor both so loosly disally'd
Thir nuptials, nor this last so trecherously
Had shorn the fatal harvest of thy head.
Is it for that such outward ornament
Was lavish't on thir Sex, that inward gifts
Were left for hast unfinish't, judgment scant,
Capacity not rais'd to apprehend
Or value what is best
 In choice, but oftest to affect the wrong?   1030
Or was too much of self-love mixt,
Of constancy no root infixt,
That either they love nothing, or not long?
 What e're it be, to wisest men and best
Seeming at first all heavenly under virgin veil,
Soft, modest, meek, demure,
Once join'd, the contrary she proves, a thorn
Intestin, far within defensive arms
A cleaving mischief, in his way to vertue
Adverse and turbulent, or by her charms   1040
Draws him awry enslav'd
With dotage, and his sense deprav'd
To folly and shameful deeds which ruin ends.
What Pilot so expert but needs must wreck
Embarqu'd with such a Stears-mate at the Helm?
 Favour'd of Heav'n who finds
One vertuous rarely found,
That in domestic good combines:
Happy that house! his way to peace is smooth:
But vertue which breaks through all opposition,   1050
And all temptation can remove,
Most shines and most is acceptable above.

1020 **Paranymph** groomsman 1025 **for that** because 1030 **affect**
prefer 1038 **Intestin** inward or domestic 1048 **combines** unites
harmoniously

Therefore Gods universal Law
Gave to the man despotic power
Over his female in due awe,
Nor from that right to part an hour,
Smile she or lowre:
So shall he least confusion draw
On his whole life, not sway'd
1060 By female usurpation, nor dismay'd.
    But had we best retire, I see a storm?
    SAM. Fair days have oft contracted wind and rain.
    CHOR. But this another kind of tempest brings.
    SAM. Be less abstruse, my riddling days are past.
    CHOR. Look now for no inchanting voice, nor fear
The bait of honied words; a rougher tongue
Draws hitherward, I know him by his stride,
The Giant *Harapha* of *Gath*, his look
Haughty as is his pile high-built and proud.
1070 Comes he in peace? what wind hath blown him hither
I less conjecture then when first I saw
The sumptuous *Dalila* floating this way:
His habit carries peace, his brow defiance.
    SAM. Or peace or not, alike to me he comes.
    CHOR. His fraught we soon shall know, he now arrives.
    HAR. I come not *Samson*, to condole thy chance,
As these perhaps, yet wish it had not been,
Though for no friendly intent. I am of *Gath*
Men call me *Harapha*, of stock renown'd
1080 As *Og* or *Anak* and the *Emims* old
That *Kiriathaim* held, thou knowst me now
If thou at all art known. Much I have heard
Of thy prodigious might and feats perform'd
Incredible to me, in this displeas'd,
That I was never present on the place
Of those encounters where we might have tri'd
Each others force in camp or listed field:
And now am come to see of whom such noise
Hath walk'd about, and each limb to survey,

1054 **despotic** absolute   1062 **contracted** brought together
1069 **pile** towering body   1074 **fraught** purpose he brings
1080 **Og, Anak, Emims** giants, Deuteronomy II: 10-11, III: 11,
Numbers XXI: 33   1081 **Kiriathaim** town where the Emims were
defeated, Genesis XIV: 5   1087 **camp** field of battle **listed** fenced
for a tournament

If thy appearance answer loud report.   1090
   SAM. The way to know were not to see but taste.
   HAR. Dost thou already single me; I thought
Gives and the Mill had tam'd thee; O that fortune
Had brought me to the field where thou art fam'd
To have wrought such wonders with an Asses Jaw;
I should have forc'd thee soon wish other arms,
Or left thy carkass where the Ass lay thrown:
So had the glory of Prowess been recover'd
To *Palestine,* won by a *Philistine*
From the unforeskinn'd race, of whom thou bear'st   1100
The highest name for valiant Acts, that honour
Certain to have won by mortal duel from thee,
I lose, prevented by thy eyes put out.
   SAM. Boast not of what thou wouldst have done, but do
What then thou would'st, thou seest it in thy hand.
   HAR. To combat with a blind man I disdain,
And thou hast need much washing to be toucht.
   SAM. Such usage as your honourable Lords
Afford me assassinated and betray'd,
Who durst not with thir whole united powers   1110
In fight withstand me single and unarm'd,
Nor in the house with chamber Ambushes
Close-banded durst attaque me, no not sleeping,
Till they had hir'd a woman with their gold
Breaking her Marriage Faith to circumvent me.
Therefore without feign'd shifts let be assign'd
Some narrow place enclos'd, where sight may give thee,
Or rather flight, no great advantage on me;
Then put on all thy gorgeous arms, thy Helmet
And Brigandine of brass, thy broad Habergeon,   1120
Vant-brass and Greves, and Gauntlet, add thy Spear
A Weavers beam, and seven-times-folded shield,
I only with an Oak'n staff will meet thee,
And raise such out-cries on thy clatter'd Iron,
Which long shall not with-hold mee from thy head,
That in a little time while breath remains thee,
Thou oft shalt wish thy self at *Gath* to boast

1092 **single** challenge to single combat 1093 **gives** gyves, fetters
1105 **hand** power 1109 **assassinated** treacherously harmed
1114 **close** secretly 1120 **Brigandine** armor of plates or rings be-
tween layers of leather **Habergeon** sleeveless coat of mail
1121 **Vant-brass, Greves** armor for forearm and shin

Again in safety what thou wouldst have done
To *Samson*, but shalt never see *Gath* more.
1130   HAR. Thou durst not thus disparage glorious arms
Which greatest Heroes have in battel worn,
Thir ornament and safety, had not spells
And black enchantments, some Magicians Art
Arm'd thee or charm'd thee strong, which thou from Heaven
Feigndst at thy birth was giv'n thee in thy hair,
Where strength can least abide, though all thy hairs
Were bristles rang'd like those that ridge the back
Of chaf't wild Boars, or ruffl'd Porcupines.
    SAM. I know no Spells, use no forbidden Arts;
1140 My trust is in the living God who gave me
At my Nativity this strength, diffus'd
No less through all my sinews, joints and bones,
Then thine, while I preserv'd these locks unshorn,
The pledge of my unviolated vow.
For proof hereof, if *Dagon* be thy god,
Go to his Temple, invocate his aid
With solemnest devotion, spread before him
How highly it concerns his glory now
To frustrate and dissolve these Magic spells,
1150 Which I to be the power of *Israel*'s God
Avow, and challenge *Dagon* to the test,
Offering to combat thee his Champion bold,
With th' utmost of his Godhead seconded:
Then thou shalt see, or rather to thy sorrow
Soon feel, whose God is strongest, thine or mine.
    HAR. Presume not on thy God, what e're he be,
Thee he regards not, owns not, hath cut off
Quite from his people, and delivered up
Into thy Enemies hand, permitted them
1160 To put out both thine eyes, and fetter'd send thee
Into the common Prison, there to grind
Among the Slaves and Asses thy comrades,
As good for nothing else, no better service
With those thy boyst'rous locks, no worthy match
For valour to assail, nor by the sword
Of noble Warriour, so to stain his honour,
But by the Barbers razor best subdu'd.
    SAM. All these indignities, for such they are
From thine, these evils I deserve and more,
1169 **thine** thy people

Acknowledge them from God inflicted on me 1170
Justly, yet despair not of his final pardon
Whose ear is ever open; and his eye
Gracious to re-admit the suppliant;
In confidence whereof I once again
Defie thee to the trial of mortal fight,
By combat to decide whose god is God,
Thine or whom I with *Israel's* Sons adore.

   Har. Fair honour that thou dost thy God, in trusting
He will accept thee to defend his cause,
A Murtherer, a Revolter, and a Robber. 1180

     Sam. Tongue-doubtie Giant, how dost thou prove me
these?

   Har. Is not thy Nation subject to our Lords?
Their Magistrates confest it, when they took thee
As a League-breaker and deliver'd bound
Into our hands: for hadst thou not committed
Notorious murder on those thirty men
At *Askalon,* who never did thee harm,
Then like a Robber stripdst them of thir robes?
The *Philistines,* when thou hadst broke the league,
Went up with armed powers thee only seeking, 1190
To others did no violence nor spoil.

    Sam. Among the Daughters of the *Philistines*
I chose a Wife, which argu'd me no foe;
And in your City held my Nuptial Feast:
But your ill-meaning Politician Lords,
Under pretence of Bridal friends and guests,
Appointed to await me thirty spies,
Who threatning cruel death constrain'd the bride
To wring from me and tell to them my secret,
That solv'd the riddle which I had propos'd. 1200
When I perceiv'd all set on enmity,
As on my enemies, where ever chanc'd,
I us'd hostility, and took thir spoil
To pay my underminers in thir coin.
My Nation was subjected to your Lords.
It was the force of Conquest; force with force
Is well ejected when the Conquer'd can.
But I a private person, whom my Countrey
As a league-breaker gave up bound, presum'd
Single Rebellion and did Hostile Acts. 1210
I was no private but a person rais'd

With strength sufficient and command from Heav'n
To free my Countrey; if their servile minds
Me their Deliverer sent would not receive,
But to thir Masters gave me up for nought,
Th' unworthier they; whence to this day they serve.
I was to do my part from Heav'n assign'd,
And had perform'd it if my known offence
Had not disabl'd me, not all your force:
1220 These shifts refuted, answer thy appellant
Though by his blindness maim'd for high attempts,
Who now defies thee thrice to single fight,
As a petty enterprise of small enforce.

 HAR. With thee a Man condemn'd, a Slave enrol'd,
Due by the Law to capital punishment?
To fight with thee no man of arms will deign.

 SAM. Cam'st thou for this, vain boaster, to survey me,
To descant on my strength, and give thy verdit?
Come nearer, part not hence so slight inform'd;
1230 But take good heed my hand survey not thee.

 HAR. O *Baal-zebub!* can my ears unus'd
Hear these dishonours, and not render death?

 SAM. No man with-holds thee, nothing from thy hand
Fear I incurable; bring up thy van,
My heels are fetter'd, but my fist is free.

 HAR. This insolence other kind of answer fits.

 SAM. Go baffl'd coward, lest I run upon thee,
Though in these chains, bulk without spirit vast,
And with one buffet lay thy structure low,
1240 Or swing thee in the Air, then dash thee down
To the hazard of thy brains and shatter'd sides.

 HAR. By *Astaroth* e're long thou shalt lament
These braveries in Irons loaden on thee.

 CHOR. His Giantship is gone somewhat crestfall'n,
Stalking with less unconsci'nable strides,
And lower looks, but in a sultrie chafe.

 SAM. I dread him not, nor all his Giant-brood,
Though Fame divulge him Father of five Sons
All of Gigantic size, *Goliah* chief.

1223 **enforce** difficulty　1228 **descant** dwell freely　1231 **Baal-zebub** Philistian god **unus'd** unaccustomed　1034 **van** advance guard　1242 **Astaroth** Canaanite goddess　1245 **unconsci'nable** unreasonable, or excessively large　1248 II Samuel xxi: 16-22, I Chronicles xx: 4-6

Chor. He will directly to the Lords, I fear,   1250
And with malitious counsel stir them up
Some way or other yet further to afflict thee.

 Sam. He must allege some cause, and offer'd fight
Will not dare mention, lest a question rise
Whether he durst accept the offer or not,
And that he durst not plain enough appear d.
Much more affliction then already felt
They cannot well impose, nor I sustain;
If they intend advantage of my labours
The work of many hands, which earns my keeping   1260
With no small profit daily to my owners.
But come what will, my deadliest foe will prove
My speediest friend, by death to rid me hence,
The worst that he can give, to me the best.
Yet so it may fall out, because thir end
Is hate, not help to me, it may with mine
Draw thir own ruin who attempt the deed.

 Chor. Oh how comely it is and how reviving
To the Spirits of just men long opprest!
When God into the hands of thir deliverer   1270
Puts invincible might
To quell the mighty of the Earth, th' oppressour,
The brute and boist'rous force of violent men
Hardy and industrious to support
Tyrannic power, but raging to pursue
The righteous and all such as honour Truth;
He all thir Ammunition
And feats of War defeats
With plain Heroic magnitude of mind
And celestial vigour arm'd,   1280
Thir Armories and Magazins contemns,
Renders them useless, while
With winged expedition
Swift as the lightning glance he executes
His errand on the wicked, who surpris'd
Lose thir defence distracted and amaz'd.

 But patience is more oft the exercise
Of Saints, the trial of thir fortitude,
Making them each his own Deliverer,
And Victor over all   1290
That tyrannie or fortune can inflict,

1283 **expedition** speed

Either of these is in thy lot,
Samson, with might endu'd
Above the Sons of men; but sight bereav'd
May chance to number thee with those
Whom Patience finally must crown.
This Idols day hath bin to thee no day of rest,
    Labouring thy mind
More then the working day thy hands,
1300 And yet perhaps more trouble is behind.
For I descry this way
Some other tending, in his hand
A Scepter or quaint staff he bears,
Comes on amain, speed in his look.
By his habit I discern him now
A Public Officer, and now at hand.
His message will be short and voluble.
    OFF. *Ebrews,* the Pris'ner *Samson* here I seek.
    CHOR. His manacles remark him, there he sits.
1310   OFF. *Samson,* to thee our Lords thus bid me say;
This day to *Dagon* is a solemn Feast,
With Sacrifices, Triumph, Pomp, and Games;
Thy strength they know surpassing human rate,
And now some public proof thereof require
To honour this great Feast, and great Assembly;
Rise therefore with all speed and come along,
Where I will see thee heartn't and fresh clad
To appear as fits before th' illustrious Lords.
    SAM. Thou knowst I am an *Ebrew,* therefore tell them,
1320 Our Law forbids at thir Religious Rites
My presence; for that cause I cannot come.
    OFF. This answer, be assur'd, will not content them.
    SAM. Have they not Sword-players, and ev'ry sort
Of Gymnic Artists, Wrestlers, Riders, Runners,
Juglers and Dancers, Antics, Mummers, Mimics,
But they must pick me out with shackles tir'd,
And over-labour'd at thir Publick Mill,
To make them sport with blind activity?
Do they not seek occasion of new quarrels
1330 On my refusal to distress me more,
Or make a game of my calamities?

1303 **quaint** curiously decorated 1307 **voluble** fluent 1309 **re-mark** mark him out 1325 **Antics** clowns **Mummers** actors in dumb-shows

Return the way thou cam'st, I will not come.
   Off. Regard thy self, this will offend them highly.
   Sam. My self? my conscience and internal peace.
Can they think me so broken, so debas'd
With corporal servitude, that my mind ever
Will condescend to such absurd commands?
Although thir drudge, to be thir fool or jester,
And in my midst of sorrow and heart-grief
To shew them feats and play before thir god,   1340
The worst of all indignities, yet on me
Joyn'd with extream contempt? I will not come.
   Off. My message was impos'd on me with speed,
Brooks no delay: is this thy resolution?
   Sam. So take it with what speed thy message needs.
   Off. I am sorry what this stoutness will produce.
   Sam. Perhaps thou shalt have cause to sorrow indeed.
   Chor. Consider, *Samson;* matters now are strain'd
Up to the highth, whether to hold or break;
He's gone, and who knows how he may report   1350
Thy words by adding fuel to the flame?
Expect another message more imperious,
More Lordly thund'ring then thou well wilt bear.
   Sam. Shall I abuse this Consecrated gift
Of strength, again returning with my hair
After my great transgression, so requite
Favour renew'd, and add a greater sin
By prostituting holy things to Idols;
A *Nazarite* in place abominable
Vaunting my strength in honour to thir *Dagon?*   1360
Besides, how vile, contemptible, ridiculous,
What act more execrably unclean, prophane?
   Chor. Yet with this strength thou serv'st the *Philistines,*
Idolatrous, uncircumcis'd, unclean.
   Sam. Not in thir Idol-worship, but by labour
Honest and lawful to deserve my food
Of those who have me in thir civil power.
   Chor. Where the heart joins not, outward acts defile not.
   Sam. Where outward force constrains, the sentence holds;
But who constrains me to the Temple of *Dagon,*   1370
Not dragging? the *Philistian* Lords command.
Commands are no constraints. If I obey them,

1342 **Joyn'd** enjoined 1346 **stoutness** arrogance 1360 **Vaunting**
displaying proudly 1369 **sentence** maxim

I do it freely; venturing to displease
God for the fear of Man, and Man prefer,
Set God behind: which in his jealousie
Shall never, unrepented, find forgiveness.
Yet that he may dispense with me or thee
Present in Temples at Idolatrous Rites
For some important cause, thou needst not doubt.

1380   CHOR. How thou wilt here come off surmounts my reach.
      SAM. Be of good courage, I begin to feel
Some rouzing motions in me which dispose
To something extraordinary my thoughts.
I with this Messenger will go along,
Nothing to do, be sure, that may dishonour
Our Law, or stain my vow of *Nazarite*.
If there be aught of presage in the mind,
This day will be remarkable in my life
By some great act, or of my days the last.

1390   CHOR. In time thou hast resolv'd, the man returns.
      OFF. Samson, this second message from our Lords
To thee I am bid say. Art thou our Slave,
Our Captive, at the public Mill our drudge,
And dar'st thou at our sending and command
Dispute thy coming? come without delay;
Or we shall find such Engines to assail
And hamper thee, as thou shalt come of force,
Though thou wert firmlier fastn'd then a rock.
      SAM. I could be well content to try thir Art,

1400 Which to no few of them would prove pernicious.
Yet knowing thir advantages too many,
Because they shall not trail me through thir streets
Like a wild Beast, I am content to go.
Masters commands come with a power resistless
To such as owe them absolute subjection;
And for a life who will not change his purpose?
(So mutable are all the ways of men)
Yet this be sure, in nothing to comply
Scandalous or forbidden in our Law.

1410   OFF. I praise thy resolution, doff these links:
By this compliance thou wilt win the Lords
To favour, and perhaps to set thee free.
      SAM. Brethren farewel, your company along

1377 **dispense with** excuse from law 1396 **Engines** instruments
of torture 1397 **hamper** fetter 1400 **pernicious** deadly

I will not wish, lest it perhaps offend them
To see me girt with Friends; and how the sight
Of me as of a common Enemy,
So dreaded once, may now exasperate them
I know not. Lords are Lordliest in thir wine;
And the well-feasted Priest then soonest fir'd
With zeal, if aught Religion seem concern'd: 1420
No less the people on thir Holy-days
Impetuous, insolent, unquenchable;
Happ'n what may, of me expect to hear
Nothing dishonourable, impure, unworthy
Our God, our Law, my Nation, or my self,
The last of me or no I cannot warrant.
    Chor. Go, and the Holy One
Of *Israel* be thy guide
To what may serve his glory best, & spread his name
Great among the Heathen round: 1430
Send thee the Angel of thy Birth, to stand
Fast by thy side, who from thy Fathers field
Rode up in flames after his message told
Of thy conception, and be now a shield
Of fire; that Spirit that first rusht on thee
In the camp of *Dan*
Be efficacious in thee now at need.
For never was from Heaven imparted
Measure of strength so great to mortal seed,
As in thy wond'rous actions hath been seen.   1440
But wherefore comes old *Manoa* in such hast
With youthful steps? much livelier then e're while
He seems: supposing here to find his Son,
Or of him bringing to us some glad news?
    Man. Peace with you brethren; my inducement hither
Was not at present here to find my Son,
By order of the Lords new parted hence
To come and play before them at thir Feast.
I heard all as I came, the City rings
And numbers thither flock, I had no will,   1450
Lest I should see him forc't to things unseemly.
But that which mov'd my coming now, was chiefly
To give ye part with me what hope I have
With good success to work his liberty.
    Chor. That hope would much rejoyce us to partake
With thee; say reverend Sire, we thirst to hear.

MAN. I have attempted one by one the Lords
Either at home, or through the high street passing,
With supplication prone and Fathers tears
1460 To accept of ransom for my Son thir pris'ner,
Some much averse I found and wondrous harsh,
Contemptuous, proud, set on revenge and spite;
That part most reverenc'd *Dagon* and his Priests,
Others more moderate seeming, but thir aim
Private reward, for which both God and State
They easily would set to sale, a third
More generous far and civil, who confess'd
They had anough reveng'd, having reduc't
Thir foe to misery beneath thir fears,
1470 The rest was magnanimity to remit,
If some convenient ransom were propos'd.
What noise or shout was that? it tore the Skie.
    CHOR. Doubtless the people shouting to behold
Thir once great.dread, captive, & blind before them,
Or at some proof of strength before them shown.
    MAN. His ransom, if my whole inheritance
May compass it, shall willingly be paid
And numberd down: much rather I shall chuse
To live the poorest in my Tribe, then richest,
1480 And he in that calamitous prison left.
No, I am fixt not to part hence without him.
For his redemption all my Patrimony,
If need be, I am ready to forgo
And quit: not wanting him, I shall want nothing.
    CHOR. Fathers are wont to lay up for thir Sons,
Thou for thy Son art bent to lay out all;
Sons wont to nurse thir Parents in old age,
Thou in old age car'st how to nurse thy Son,
Made older then thy age through eye-sight lost.
1490   MAN. It shall be my delight to tend his eyes,
And view him sitting in the house, enobl'd
With all those high exploits by him atchiev'd,
And on his shoulders waving down those locks,
That of a Nation arm'd the strength contain'd:
And I perswade me God had not permitted
His strength again to grow up with his hair
Garrison'd round about him like a Camp
Of faithful Souldiery, were not his purpose
To use him further yet in some great service,

Not to sit idle with so great a gift   1500
Useless, and thence ridiculous about him.
And since his strength with eye-sight was not lost,
God will restore him eye-sight to his strength.

   CHOR. Thy hopes are not ill founded nor seem vain
Of his delivery, and thy joy thereon
Conceiv'd, agreeable to a Fathers love,
In both which we, as next participate.

   MAN. I know your friendly minds and—O what noise!
Mercy of Heav'n what hideous noise was that!
Horribly loud unlike the former shout.   1510

   CHOR. Noise call you it or universal groan
As if the whole inhabitation perish'd,
Blood, death, and deathful deeds are in that noise,
Ruin, destruction at the utmost point.

   MAN. Of ruin indeed methought I heard the noise,
Oh it continues, they have slain my Son.

   CHOR. Thy Son is rather slaying them, that outcry
From slaughter of one foe could not ascend.

   MAN. Some dismal accident it needs must be;
What shall we do, stay here or run and see?   1520

   CHOR. Best keep together here, lest running thither
We unawares run into dangers mouth.
This evil on the *Philistines* is fall'n,
From whom could else a general cry be heard?
The sufferers then will scarce molest us here,
From other hands we need not much to fear.
What if his eye-sight (for to *Israels* God
Nothing is hard) by miracle restor'd,
He now be dealing dole among his foes,
And over heaps of slaughter'd walk his way?   1530

   MAN. That were a joy presumptuous to be thought.

   CHOR. Yet God hath wrought things as incredible
For his people of old; what hinders now?

   MAN. He can I know, but doubt to think he will;
Yet Hope would fain subscribe, and tempts Belief.
A little stay will bring some notice hither.

   CHOR. Of good or bad so great, of bad the sooner;
For evil news rides post, while good news baits.
And to our wish I see one hither speeding,
An *Ebrew,* as I guess, and of our Tribe.   1540

1506 **agreeable** suitable 1507 **next** connected by birth 1529 **dole**
grief 1538 **baits** delays

Mess. O whither shall I run, or which way flie
The sight of this so horrid spectacle
Which earst my eyes beheld and yet behold;
For dire imagination still persues me.
But providence or instinct of nature seems,
Or reason though disturb'd, and scarse consulted
To have guided me aright, I know not how,
To thee first reverend *Manoa*, and to these
My Countreymen, whom here I knew remaining,
1550 As at some distance from the place of horrour,
So in the sad event too much concern'd.
    Man. The accident was loud, & heard before thee
With rueful cry, yet what it was we hear not,
No Preface needs, thou seest we long to know.
    Mess. It would burst forth, but I recover breath
And sense distract, to know well what I utter.
    Man. Tell us the sum, the circumstance defer.
    Mess. *Gaza* yet stands, but all her Sons are fall'n,
All in a moment overwhelm'd and fall'n.
1560   Man. Sad, but thou knowst to *Israelites* not saddest
The desolation of a Hostile City.
    Mess. Feed on that first, there may in grief be surfet.
    Man. Relate by whom. Mess. By *Samson*.
        Man. That still lessens
The sorrow, and converts it nigh to joy.
    Mess. Ah *Manoa* I refrain, too suddenly
To utter what will come at last too soon;
Lest evil tidings with too rude irruption
Hitting thy aged ear should pierce too deep.
    Man. Suspense in news is torture, speak them out.
1570   Mess. Then take the worst in brief, *Samson* is dead.
    Man. The worst indeed, O all my hope's defeated
To free him hence! but death who sets all free
Hath paid his ransom now and full discharge.
What windy joy this day had I conceiv'd
Hopeful of his Delivery, which now proves
Abortive as the first-born bloom of spring
Nipt with the lagging rear of winters frost.
Yet e're I give the rains to grief, say first,
How dy'd he? death to life is crown or shame.
1580 All by him fell thou say'st, by whom fell he,
What glorious hand gave *Samson* his deaths wound?
1543 **earst** just now

MESS. Unwounded of his enemies he fell.
MAN. Wearied with slaughter then or how? explain.
MESS. By his own hands. MAN. Self-violence? what cause
Brought him so soon at variance with himself
Among his foes? MESS. Inevitable cause
At once both to destroy and be destroy'd;
The Edifice where all were met to see him
Upon thir heads and on his own he pull'd.
    MAN. O lastly over-strong against thy self!   1590
A dreadful way thou took'st to thy revenge.
More then anough we know; but while things yet
Are in confusion, give us if thou canst,
Eye-witness of what first or last was done,
Relation more particular and distinct.
    MESS. Occasions drew me early to this City,
And as the gates I enter'd with Sun-rise,
The morning Trumpets Festival proclaim'd
Through each high street: little I had dispatch't
When all abroad was rumour'd that this day   1600
Samson should be brought forth to shew the people
Proof of his mighty strength in feats and games;
I sorrow'd at his captive state, but minded
Not to be absent at that spectacle.
The building was a spacious Theatre
Half round on two main Pillars vaulted high,
With seats where all the Lords and each degree
Of sort, might sit in order to behold,
The other side was op'n, where the throng
On banks and scaffolds under Skie might stand;   1610
I among these aloof obscurely stood.
The Feast and noon grew high, and Sacrifice
Had fill'd thir hearts with mirth, high chear, & wine,
When to thir sports they turn'd. Immediately
Was *Samson* as a public servant brought,
In thir state Livery clad; before him Pipes
And Timbrels, on each side went armed guards,
Both horse and foot before him and behind
Archers, and Slingers, Cataphracts and Spears.
At sight of him the people with a shout   1620
Rifted the Air clamouring thir god with praise,

1596 **Occasions** affairs of business   1603 **minded** resolved   1607-8
degree Of sort rank of nobility   1610 **banks** benches   1616 **Livery**
dress of servants   1619 **Cataphracts** cavalrymen on armored horses

Who had made thir dreadful enemy thir thrall.
He patient but undaunted where they led him,
Came to the place, and what was set before him
Which without help of eye, might be assay'd,
To heave, pull, draw, or break, he still perform'd
All with incredible, stupendous force,
None daring to appear Antagonist.
At length for intermission sake they led him
1630 Between the pillars; he his guide requested
(For so from such as nearer stood we heard)
As over-tir'd to let him lean a while
With both his arms on those two massie Pillars
That to the arched roof gave main support.
He unsuspitious led him; which when *Samson*
Felt in his arms, with head a while enclin'd,
And eyes fast fixt he stood, as one who pray'd,
Or some great matter in his mind revolv'd.
At last with head erect thus cryed aloud,
1640 Hitherto, Lords, what your commands impos'd
I have perform'd, as reason was, obeying,
Not without wonder or delight beheld.
Now of my own accord such other tryal
I mean to shew you of my strength, yet greater;
As with amaze shall strike all who behold.
This utter'd, straining all his nerves he bow'd,
As with the force of winds and waters pent,
When Mountains tremble, those two massie Pillars
With horrible convulsion to and fro,
1650 He tugg'd, he shook, till down they came and drew
The whole roof after them, with burst of thunder
Upon the heads of all who sate beneath,
Lords, Ladies, Captains, Councellors, or Priests,
Thir choice nobility and flower, not only
Of this but each *Philistian* City round
Met from all parts to solemnize this Feast.
Samson with these immixt, inevitably
Pulld down the same destruction on himself;
The vulgar only scap'd who stood without.
1660   Chor. O dearly-bought revenge, yet glorious!
Living or dying thou hast fulfill'd
The work for which thou wast foretold
To *Israel,* and now ly'st victorious

1646 **nerves** sinews 1659 **vulgar** ordinary folk

Among thy slain self-kill'd
Not willingly, but tangl'd in the fold
Of dire necessity, whose law in death conjoin'd
Thee with thy slaughter'd foes in number more
Then all thy life had slain before.

SEMICHOR. While thir hearts were jocund and sublime,
Drunk with Idolatry, drunk with Wine,   1670
And fat regorg'd of Bulls and Goats,
Chaunting thir Idol, and preferring
Before our living Dread who dwells
In *Silo* his bright Sanctuary:
Among them he a spirit of phrenzie sent,
Who hurt thir minds,
And urg'd them on with mad desire
To call in hast for thir destroyer;
They only set on sport and play
Unweetingly importun'd   1680
Thir own destruction to come speedy upon them.
So fond are mortal men
Fall'n into wrath divine,
As thir own ruin on themselves to invite,
Insensate left, or to sense reprobate,
And with blindness internal struck.

SEMICHOR. But he though blind of sight,
Despis'd and thought extinguish't quite,
With inward eyes illuminated
His fierie vertue rouz'd   1690
From under ashes into sudden flame,
And as an ev'ning Dragon came,
Assailant on the perched roosts,
And nests in order rang'd
Of tame villatic Fowl; but as an Eagle
His cloudless thunder bolted on thir heads.
So vertue giv'n for lost,
Deprest, and overthrown, as seem'd,
Like that self-begott'n bird
In the *Arabian* woods embost,   1700
That no second knows nor third,

1669 sublime exalted 1674 Silo Shiloh, Exodus XL: 34 1680 un-
weetingly unknowingly 1692 Dragon serpent 1695 villatic
farmyard 1699 self-begott'n bird the Phoenix, a mythical bird
supposed to die in fire and to be reborn out of its own ashes
1700 embost sheltered in a thicket

And lay e're while a Holocaust,
From out her ashie womb now teem'd,
Revives, reflourishes, then vigorous most
When most unactive deem'd,
And though her body die, her fame survives,
A secular bird ages of lives.

    MAN. Come, come, no time for lamentation now,
Nor much more cause, *Samson* hath quit himself
1710 Like *Samson,* and heroicly hath finish'd
A life Heroic, on his Enemies
Fully reveng'd, hath left them years of mourning,
And lamentation to the Sons of *Caphtor*
Through all *Philistian* bounds. To *Israel*
Honour hath left, and freedom, let but them
Find courage to lay hold on this occasion,
To himself and Fathers house eternal fame;
And which is best and happiest yet, all this
With God not parted from him, as was feard,
1720 But favouring and assisting to the end.
Nothing is here for tears, nothing to wail
Or knock the breast, no weakness, no contempt,
Dispraise, or blame, nothing but well and fair,
And what may quiet us in a death so noble.
Let us go find the body where it lies
Sok't in his enemies blood, and from the stream
With lavers pure and cleansing herbs wash off
The clotted gore. I with what speed the while
(*Gaza* is not in plight to say us nay)
1730 Will send for all my kindred, all my friends
To fetch him hence and solemnly attend
With silent obsequie and funeral train
Home to his Fathers house: there will I build him
A Monument, and plant it round with shade
Of Laurel ever green, and branching Palm,
With all his Trophies hung, and Acts enroll'd
In copious Legend, or sweet Lyric Song.
Thither shall all the valiant youth resort,
And from his memory inflame thir breasts
1740 To matchless valour, and adventures high:
The Virgins also shall on feastful days

1702 **Holocaust** sacrifice consumed by fire 1707 **secular living**
for centuries 1709 **quit** acquitted 1713 **sons of Caphtor** Philis-
tines, Deuteronomy II: 23

Visit his Tomb with flowers, only bewailing
His lot unfortunate in nuptial choice,
From whence captivity and loss of eyes.
    CHOR. All is`best, though we oft doubt,
What th' unsearchable dispose
Of highest wisdom brings about,
And ever best found in the close.
Oft he seems to hide his face,
But unexpectedly returns   1750
And to his faithful Champion hath in place
Bore witness gloriously; whence *Gaza* mourns
And all that band them to resist
His uncontroulable intent,
His servants he with new acquist
Of true experience from this great event
With peace and consolation hath dismist,
And calm of mind all passion spent.

1755 **acquist** acquisition

SELECTED BIBLIOGRAPHY

Bush, D., *English Literature in the Earlier Seventeenth Century,* rev. ed., New York, Oxford, 1962.

———, *Mythology and the Renaissance Tradition,* rev. ed., New York, Norton, 1963.

———, *John Milton,* New York, Macmillan, 1964.

Hanford, J. H., *A Milton Handbook,* 4th ed., New York, Appleton-Century-Crofts, 1954.

Hutchinson, F. E., *Milton and the English Mind,* New York, Collier, 1962.

Nicolson, M. H., *John Milton,* New York, Farrar, Straus, 1963.

Svendsen, K., *Milton and Science,* Cambridge, Harvard, 1957.

Haller, W., *The Rise of Puritanism,* New York, Columbia, 1938.

Barker, A. E., *Milton and the Puritan Dilemma,* Toronto, Toronto, 1942, 1964.

Hanford, J. H., "The Youth of Milton," *Studies in Shakespeare, Milton and Donne, University of Michigan Publications in Language and Literature,* I (1925), 89-163.

Woodhouse, A. S. P., "Notes on Milton's Early Development," *U. of Toronto Quarterly,* XIII (1943), 66-101.

Allen, D. C., *The Harmonious Vision,* Baltimore, Johns Hopkins, 1954.

Tuve, R., *Images and Themes in Five Poems by Milton,* Cambridge, Harvard, 1957.

Brett, R. L., *Reason and Imagination,* New York, Oxford, 1960.

Prince, F. T., *The Italian Element in Milton's Verse,* Oxford, Clarendon, 1954.

Finney, G. L., *Musical Backgrounds for English Literature,* New Brunswick, Rutgers, 1962.

Barker, A. E., ed., *Milton: Modern Essays in Criticism,* New York, Oxford, 1965. Essays by various hands, otherwise unlisted here, on earlier and later poems.

Barker, A. E., "The Pattern of Milton's Nativity Ode," *U. of Toronto Quarterly,* X, 1941, 167-181.

Broadbent, J. B., "The Nativity Ode," *The Living Milton,* ed. F. Kermode, London, Routledge, 1961.

Nelson, L., Jr., "Milton's Nativity Ode," *Baroque Lyric Poetry,* New Haven, Yale, 1961.

Brooks, C., "The Light Symbolism in *L'Allegro* and *Il Penseroso,*" *The Well Wrought Urn,* New York, Reynal, 1947.

Leishman, J. B., "*L'Allegro* and *Il Penseroso* . . .", *Essays and Studies,* IV, 1951, 1-36.

Carpenter, N. C., "The Place of Music in *L'Allegro* and *Il Penseroso,*" *U. of Toronto Quarterly,* XXII, 1953, 354-367.

Tate, E., "Milton's *L'Allegro* and *Il Penseroso* . . .", *Modern Language Notes,* LXXVI, 1961, 585-590.

Woodhouse, A. S. P., "The Argument of Milton's *Comus,*" *U. of Toronto Quarterly,* XI, 1941, 48-71.

Sensabaugh, G. F., "The Milieu of *Comus,*" *Studies in Philology,* XLI, 1944, 233-249.

Seaton, E., "*Comus* and Shakespeare," *Essays and Studies,* XXXI, 1946, 68-80.

Arthos, J., *On a Mask . . . at Ludlow Castle,* Ann Arbor, Michigan, 1954.

Madsen, W. G., "*Comus,*" *Three Studies in the Renaissance, Yale Studies in English,* 138, 1958, 185-218.

Patrides, C. A., ed., *Milton's "Lycidas"* . . . , New York, Holt, Rinehart and Winston, 1961. Essays, not otherwise listed here, by various hands.

Mayerson, C. W., "The Orpheus Image in *Lycidas,*" *Publications of the Modern Language Association,* LXIV, 1949, 189-207.

Madsen, W. G., "The Voice of Michael in *Lycidas,*" *Studies in English Literature,* III, 1963, 1-7.

Woodhouse, A. S. P., "Milton's Pastoral Monodies," *Studies in Honour of G. Norwood,* ed. M. E. White, Toronto, Toronto, 1952.

Hanford, J. H., "The Arrangement and Order of Milton's Sonnets," *Modern Philology,* XVIII, 1921, 475-483.

Stoehr, T., "Syntax and Form in Milton's Sonnets," *English Studies*, XLV, 1964, 289-301.

Robins, H. F., "Milton's First Sonnet on his Blindness," *Review of English Studies*, VII, 1956, 360-366.

Slakey, R. L., "Milton's Sonnet on his Blindness," *English Literary History*, XXVIII, 1960, 122-130.

Wheeler, T., "Milton's Twenty-third Sonnet," *Studies in Philology*, LVIII, 1961, 510-515.

Hanford, J. H., "*Samson Agonistes* and Milton in Old Age," *Studies in Shakespeare, Milton and Donne, U. of Michigan Publications in Language and Literature*, I, 1925, 167-189.

Jebb, R. C., "*Samson Agonistes* and the Hellenic Drama," *Proceedings of the British Academy*, III, 1907-8, 341-348.

Parker, W. R., *Milton's Debt to Greek Tragedy in "Samson Agonistes,"* Baltimore, Johns Hopkins, 1937.

Krouse, F. M., *Milton's Samson and the Christian Tradition,* Princeton, Princeton, 1949.

Stein, A., *Heroic Knowledge: An Interpretation of . . . "Samson Agonistes,"* Minneapolis, Minnesota, 1957.

Bowra, C. M., *"Samson Agonistes," Inspiration and Poetry,* London, Macmillan, 1955.

Gossman, A., "Milton's Samson and the Tragic Hero . . .", *Journal of English and Germanic Philology*, LXVI, 1962, 528-534.

Chambers, A. B. "Wisdom and Fortitude in *Samson Agonistes*," *Publications of the Modern Language Association*, LXXVIII, 1963, 315-320.

Barker, A. E., "Structural and Doctrinal Pattern in Milton's Later Poems," *Essays in English Literature . . . ,* ed. M. MacLure and F. W. Watt, Toronto, Toronto, 1964.